# Characters of the Sacred

## The World of Archetypal Drama

# Characters of the Sacred

## The World of Archetypal Drama

Bill Pearlman

Foreword by
Daniel C. Noel

duende press
placitas, new mexico

## ACKNOWLEDGMENTS

I'd like to particularly thank colleagues Ron Frost, Mark and Maxine Rossman, and Fred Zook of Ottawa University in Phoenix who were instrumental in the development of the original graduate program in Archetypal Drama Therapy. For its most recent incarnation at Southwestern College in Santa Fe, I want to thank Marylou Butler, Katherine Ninos and Robert Waterman. For a wealth of ideas and supportive conversation I'd like to acknowledge Peter Marin, Charles Whitt, Lou Rosenberg, Dick Hopkins, Howard McConeghey, Adam Blatner, Dorothy Satten, Sandy Poling, Mara Sidoli, Renaldo Fischer, Rebecca Peterson, Katy Power, Denise Chartrand and Bill Bulay. And a special salute to friends at the Institute for the Study of the Imagination/Southwest, and to Tom Moore who founded the original prototype for ISI. For support in employing archetypal drama in a hospital setting, I'd like to acknowledge patients and staff at Charter Hospital of Albuquerque. At Prescott College, thanks go out to Mary Grace Lentz. For help with the manuscript and the patience to bear with the entire project, grateful and heartfelt thanks to Larry and Lenore Goodell of Duende Press. And to the numerous students who have come to the work with continuous enthusiasm, I send a grateful shiver of joy and hopes for the progress of your lives and work.


ISBN 0-915008-50-5

duende press

po box 571 placitas, new mexico 87043

# ꕤ CONTENTS ꕤ

# FOREWORD

I'm not a drama therapist, but as a college teacher in the academic field of religious studies, specializing in the psychology of religion and in correlations of religion with the arts, I am deeply concerned to explore what Jung's psychology has called "the archetypal " and what religion scholars have termed "the sacred." And these phenomena, I have found, manifest themselves as often in the arts as under institutional religious auspices. It was therefore with great excitement that I read about the new/old avenues of exploration, experiential as well as intellectual, that Bill Pearlman has opened up for us in his important work.

The reader of *Characters of the Sacred* will find here "dramatic testimony" to the power of his innovative approach to drama therapy. Drawing on the psychodrama tradition of Moreno together with acting theories and techniques from Stanislavski, Brook, and Grotowski, Bill uniquely weds these rich resources to the school of archetypal or imaginal psychology.

This latter direction in psychological thought and therapy extends Jung's emphasis on this reality of psyche's (soul's) imaginings, taking his "psychological faith" to a new level of commitment related to James Hlllman's conviction that the mind has a "poetic basis." The mind, or the soul, in this view, produces images as a poet would and as its native, or self-defining, activity. These images are likewise seen as real presences with which (or with whom) the ego must enter into dialogue for anything like a creative identity, a soulful selfhood, to result. Jung foresaw this, Hillman formulated it, and Thomas Moore has facilitated it with his skillful popularizations.

Bill Pearlman now brings a significantly new modality to this effort of inner dialogue. He names it Archetypal Drama Therapy, and it deserves to be considered by all who care for soul, who seek to cultivate, as Moore would put it, "depth and Sacredness" in their lives. This is, if you will, the Shamanism at the heart of "show business," where what is shown are inhabitants of another world that impinges on our own through the emotions of both dailiness and dreams.

Here my own interests strongly converge with Bill's: he valuably reminds us of the religious—or, more specifically, the ritual—roots of drama. He thus shows us how the sacred, invoked and served on the stages of ancient Greece, can again be at hand in the soul-making community of this "theater of therapy." Such a community, it should be stressed, is an inner or imaginal assemblage made external in the medium of embodied actors and their actions, including their impassioned speech. Bill's enterprise therefore supplements in an extremely helpful fashion the "active imagination" method Jung developed to allow for an even-handed conversation between the ego and the deep psyche.

As a trained actor Bill knows how to engage the imagining soul *actively*. This he imparts to his therapy groups in the context of casting characters and empowering their spontaneous performance. A group in action—as I have observed when Bill leads them—gives unusual attention to the dynamics of the inner dialogue, the movements of its imaginal figures made manifest in the safe and, it may be, sacred space of the therapy room.

The descriptions and discussions of all this in *Characters of the Sacred* often serve to place the reader in that room too. Bill Pearlman, also a poet, here gives us language that not only informs but evokes, voicing his world of archetypal drama in a way that invites us in.

I am delighted and enlightened for having accepted his invitation.

DANIEL C. NOEL, Ph.D.

# ❧ PREFACE ☙

As a preface, I'm going to briefly take you into the world of archetypal drama from the perspective of allowing you to see what would be happening if you were there: There is a process unfolding that is one of intrinsic freshness. We are entering a spontaneous world in which there is no particular foreknowledge of what will transpire. Nothing is established: neither subject matter nor order of worker. Neither who will speak first nor the way the occasion will be presented. The director will welcome everyone and then:

*The atmosphere is one of readiness. Soon we will be underway, the words will be translated into action. The issues: children, destiny, marriage, love, ambivalence, the future, the past, the way the imaginal road might open up if we were to embark in that particular direction. The spirit world beckons. As does the world of archetypal drama. Am I looking at my condition in the right way? Is there something I'm missing? We are moving into fresh territory. Potential characters are beginning to stir in our personal and collective depths.*

*

For many years, I worked as a theatre actor while also practicing therapy. There has been in my discovery and development of archetypal drama therapy a way of being in the world that is full of promise. The work anchors us to a broad landscape of love and to the unfolding power of dramatic truth. What continues to be remarkable about the work is that it is deeply tied to the heart of theatre while heading out into remarkable therapeutic territory. It is a developmental process that has about it a triumphant gleam, full of promise as a tool for various levels of practice and research. It is above all an experience that has a breadth that captures a whole range of pivotal human concerns.

Jungian analysis has taught me a great deal about my own identity. In analysis, the inner world comes alive as the investigation of dreams and the capacity for imaginative thinking matures. Walt Whitman's "I contain multitudes" comes back as deeply true when it comes to analytic work. And Jung felt that analytical work had parallels in alchemy. The alchemist worked on his materials as he worked on himself, on his own soul. In the drama workshops, you begin to take your own dramatic potential seriously. You form bridges and alliances in which other people (in role) enter into dramatic co-operation with you. Most members of the drama workshops I have led are able to enter in at various levels, sometimes as helpers, always as supportive audience. The audience in the workshop is the group itself. It is a self-contained dramatic troupe, with all the inner capacities (in the Stanislavskian sense) to make theatre 'live.' And that is always the test of theatre work: does it live? Is there a vitality in it that breaks new ground, that gives us new emotional and imaginative experience?

Archetypal therapy is about the soul and it is about how art and life can blend to make a new synthesis. This book is about many things. It is about art therapy, particularly archetypal drama therapy, and it is about how the soul comes to be at home in the world of archetypal drama. The project involves many supportive casts: my students and colleagues at The Institute for Archetypal Drama (New Mexico), Ottawa University (Phoenix), Prescott College (Prescott), and Southwestern College (Santa Fe); friends and co-directors in so many enterprising struggles in both life and art; directors I've worked with; theatres I've played in; the deep camaraderie that extends ideas into palpable joys; and the recurrent theme of communal life, its paramount yield the embodiment of a spirit of sharing that often rises to a transcendence suggesting the miraculous. Throughout the book, I will present examples of the work as it is often experienced in the workshops. This will usually take the form of either a short vignette or a partially reconstructed dialogue in which the names of participants have been changed to ensure anonymity. We should not forget the writers whose works helped shape ideas for the core of this work: C.G. Jung, James Hillman, Erik Erikson, J.L. Moreno, Henry Corbin, Jerzy Grotowski and so many others. I feel as though there has been a sense of purpose here that joins up with an animated team of imaginal adventurers whose multi-voiced creative spree has changed our way of thinking about therapy, art and the world within and around us.

*

In brief, archetypal drama therapy involves a group of persons gathered under the direction of a leader to explore relevant issues in a spontaneous dramatic context. We are open to any material individuals present, but we are particularly interested in themes that enter what we call the archetypal or transpersonal, so that we can cast and dramatize universal themes, allowing the dramatic piece to enter the collective domain where there is an expansive imaginative territory, where the soul can roam in its own boundless eternity.

Placitas, New Mexico — BILL PEARLMAN

*What an archetypal drama of death and rebirth lies hidden in the coniunctio, and what immemorial human emotions clash together in this problem. It is the moral task of alchemy to bring the feminine, maternal background of the masculine psyche, seething with passions, into harmony with the principle of the spirit—truly a labour of Hercules!* (*Mysterium Coniunctionis,* C.G. Jung)

*PSYCHOLOGY must be gained for it is not given, and without psychological education we do not understand ourselves and we make our daimons suffer. This suggests that a reason for psychotherapy of whatever school and for whatever complaint is to gain psychology—a logos of the soul that is at the same moment a therepeia of soul. We need to gain the intelligent response that makes the soul intelligible, a craft and order that understands it, a knowledgeable deftness that cares for its wants in speech. And if logos is its therapy, because it articulates the psyche's wants, then one answer to what the soul wants is psychology. (Healing Fiction,* James Hillman)

*I DO BELIEVE that the secret longing and ultimate ambition of all theatre is to return to the bosom of the ritual out of which—in both the pagan and the Christian world—it sprang. (Essays,* Thomas Mann)

# ℘ 1 ℘
# THE FESTIVE WELLSPRINGS OF ARCHETYPAL DRAMA

*And it seems to us that one of the principal functions of all art is precisely to set in motion the archetypal reality of the transpersonal within the individual and on the highest level of artistic experience to bring the individual himself to transcendence—that is, to raise him above time and epoch and also above the limited eternity realized in any limited archetypal form—to lead him to the timeless radiant dynamic that is at the heart of the world. (Art and the Creative Unconscious,* Erich Neumann)

In our work in Archetypal Drama, we have found that the archetypal world has an informational resonance when we activate it, and whether we are talking about traditional archetypal figures such as the magician, the poet, the lover, the wise old man or personified ideas like fear, courage, rage, intimacy and many others, the essential factor is that we are entering parts of the collective psyche in which there is a great deal of energy. We can think of the archetype as an inborn potentiality, an ancient internality based in a constantly recurring situation. And experience has shown that tapping into this personified realm through dialogue can be very helpful to persons stuck in obstructive conditions where the ego is wrestling with its own shadow in a losing situation. The challenge is to take on these forces and see if there can be some kind of imaginal communication or transcendence on terms other than the ego's defensive attempts to dominate the action. One could argue that the dramatic staging allows for an expanded condition in which to play out the psyche's deepest purposes. This usually calls the entire psyche into action and involves the domain of dialogue as an advanced instrument of creative communication.

In shaping a therapeutic activity which blends ideas from Jungian and Archetypal Psychology as well as from psychodrama and the dramatic arts, it's been a great help in finding raw material from diverse authors who have experimented and thought about what I'm attempting, and have broken ground that I now find useful. The field is vast and not limited to one camp. It involves historical perspectives on ritual, the creative-expressive therapies, psychopathologies, the archaic metaphorical ground of the archetype, the theatre and its modernist traditions (especially in the work of Grotowski, Artaud and Brook), and a whole range of ideas related to spontaneous group ceremony devoted to instruction and celebration.

*

*The deepest roots of theater's special ability to create that 'festive' sense of community also lie on something...which grows out of the ancient essence of theater as ritual. It is a kind of immediate and vivid enactment of the very mystery of human existence. (Letters to Olga,* Vaclav Havel)

Psychodrama was first developed by Jacob Moreno in Vienna in the 1920s and has been expanded into various areas by numerous practitioners. My scope here involves the fresh perspective that my own background in Jung's and Hillman's ideas brings to this ongoing concern: to find in the drama a therapeutic and imaginal structure alongside the theatre's ancient festive potential. For those of us who as actors, writers and directors know the theatre and its capacities, this book is an extension of ideas often experienced in the theatre but largely unknown to others, including most psychotherapists. The wellspring that leads to the world of archetypal drama is the theatre itself and follows Havel's idea of theatre's 'special ability' to create a sense of community that goes to the heart of human aspiration. I have often felt over many years' involvement in both therapy and theatre that the theatre has attracted people who went into it for its inherent capacity to heal, so that we could argue that the drama has always been a home base for healers. But for those many actors who have not had a satisfying professional acting career, this work can be helpful in deploying your talents in a new direction. The drama pre-dates what we call therapy, and has always had about its core a splendid ability to transform human concerns into resolution and affirmation.

*

This book is an effort to find a language and method of practice in the broad realm of the psychology of art that has deep roots in western culture and in the work of Jung, Hillman, Corbin, Watkins, Lawrence and others who have inquired deeply into the subject of art's relation to soul. The destined purpose is that this will prove useful to students, artists and practical workers in realms of the soul. By soul I mean that recurrent psychical depth that asks us to pay imaginative attention to our own processes in all their complexity and richness.

In addition to inquiring into philosophical antecedents to archetypal drama, I will also offer my own inner experience with this work as well as reports based on the work of students and participants in my workshops. It's my sense that the actual work has a specificity and meaning that helps establish the coherency and value of theory. And the work that occurs spontaneously in the workshops in Archetypal Drama have interesting parallels to the creative spirit that enters realms of inspiration and prophecy long associated with our most important artistic achievements. Characters graced with a sacred aspect have long appeared in the theatre, and what we are after was particularly active in medieval morality plays in which a whole range of personified figures (Virtue, Sin, Redemption, Glory, etc.) inhabited the religious dramas.

A word should be said about the healing capacity of artistic expression. In our workshops, there are parallels between improvisational work and the kind of spontaneous events that occur when persons are considering their most important issues. We start by asking the group members how they are, what is actually going on inside them. Each person has the chance to locate her mood, idea, image or possible course of work. Each person has the choice of working as a protagonist (the leading part), or as an auxiliary (supporting player), or simply as an observer. There is no pressure to perform. The group might also choose a lengthy warmup, doing acting exercises such as mirroring or empty chair dialogues. Spontaneity is at the heart of it, regaining the ability to play meaningfully in the unfolding presence of the dramatic moment.

The workshops in archetypal drama are capable of restoring the dignity and vitality of theatre at its best. Our workshop is primarily a spontaneous theatre, an instant theatre, but its presence of mind comes from its ability to find in raw inner material—namely dreams, fantasies, myths, hunches and imaginative ideas—the basis for pursuing a dramatically therapeutic action. And the action in the workshops is as varied as the world is. Sometimes we find a single dream image and run with it; sometimes we go into a personal relationship and find various threads that lead back to the imagination of a world just beginning to unfold. Sometimes the dream world is adjacent to another more conscious world and we can see how the two blend or refuse to blend, creating perhaps an imbalance or an ambivalence that must be examined. And the stories that lie buried in us can come alive and we can make use of that energy that comes from the treasure of archetypal images stored perhaps for a long time in the unconscious. And the work is often keyed to finding a new direction or a new archetypal energy, or understanding blockage or seeing the vitality of a dream image that heretofore was lost. It is a coming back to take another look at what we are, in the shared atmosphere of a fresh stage where a new communion is not only possible, but is often asking to be born.

In the workshops, we live through various stages of transformation. Each transition—whether adolescence, love, maturity or old age—has its unique demands and essential forces. But the theatre event, or the will to compensate the crisis with dramatic achievement, becomes in our work a way to find a place to both enact the problem and transform it. The work gives the individual who is in the throes of a conflict or a constellated complex a chance to start off on a productive path; it gives her a rallying activity that rouses the very quick of her. The work becomes a solution—to borrow an expression from Robert Musil—to what is. And hopefully the entire ensemble finds meaning that is pursued and produced in the act of creation. This entry into the creative world—combined with the empowering capacity to explore it in dramatic form—is where the healing begins.

When I was considering how the archetypes might interweave with dramatic action, the recurring sense was that we were dealing with intensely relevant personifications in both realms. As Jung says: "As the archetypes, like all numinous contents, are relatively autonomous, they require a dialectical procedure, a real coming to terms with them, often conducted in a dialogue form.... Usually the process runs a dramatic course." (*Collected Works* 9, Part 1)

As in traditional Morenean psychodrama (with its core group of protagonist, auxiliaries, doubles and observers), each dramatic event is directed and cast. The director will ask the group: "who is willing to help the protagonist?" and "who would prefer to merely observe?" When everyone is willing to help, then when a particular entity, person or image needs an embodied form, the director will ask the person "to choose someone to play this image." And the casting can go on throughout the drama. Group size varies, but we have found that somewhere between 8 and 12 persons is an ideal size group, and seems to allow both the diversity and intimacy that the creative enterprise demands. What traditional psychodrama calls the double or alter-ego, we generally change to what we call "an inner companion." This has historical analogues in the chorus of Greek drama, which has the role of essential resonance or dialogue with the protagonist.

**The world of archetypal drama brings to the fore the artistic struggle to bring form out of chaos, giving it new communicative design, plunging into memory and desire, image and archetype. Opposites combine, ego and archetype reverse roles, Lear and his Fool collide in spontaneous uprising, Nora and Helmer divorce in broad stage light, Othello's jealous rage is given the safe freedoms of enclosed theatrical space, The Shadow is given the chance to mewl its dense irrational tones, The Great Mother is glad to be unhappy, transcendent and mild, The Magician extolls the virtues of ambiguity and endless miracle, The Puer brags about The Road and the persistent adventures of new life, new love, the vanishing act that always brings fresh sensation.**

We find in the dramatic interaction of the archetypal and the personal something that draws us in, giving a refuge, a creative home for our desire to be heard on the stage, to be discovered with our multiple dramatic parts exposed. Psychotherapy has always emphasized dialogue between individuals; the client has a story to tell and the therapist as compassionate listener becomes the attentive audience. And the client has a huge range of freedom of expression: there are no restrictions as to subject matter or feeling: dreams, fears, senses not yet verbalized—it's all possible. And having these inner events and stories heard is intrinsically therapeutic, it gives us a foundation for new directions our lives might take. In the archetypal drama setting, everyone gets the opportunity to play multiple roles, sometimes listening to another, sometimes entering into a personal dramatic event and sometimes being in the heart of the emotional "soup," feeling one's way to another level of understanding.

In another vein, the relationship between dramatic therapy and various forms of ritual associated with the drama is an interesting one, and one that we will take up in chapters ahead. Jung has studied the phenomenon of ritual in various contexts, none to me so poignant as his study of the sacrifice of the Mass where he talks about the mass as a mystery drama that represents the sacrifice and resurrection of Christ, not as a repetition of historical event, but as an event paradoxically enacting the original event in a unique 'moment of eternity in time.' (see CW 9, Part 1, p. 117)

*

In our workshops there is sometimes simultaneously a present experience and another dimension that contains an often timeless quality, so that we speak of a special kind of time, or sacred time (Eliade). And this confluence of special conditions has always been a part of theatre work. The various degrees of participation that Jung mentions above also occur in the drama. As in Grotowski's theatre, in archetypal drama the audience is cast in significant roles, for the audience is really the group which has met for artistic/therapeutic purposes. And this often generates a human event that surpasses any kind of aesthetic purposiveness. It is all within the context of dramatic artifice and the play of consciousness and yet it surpasses all that and transcends category. It becomes an affirmation of existence, of relationship, of watched and watcher, of spectator and actor, of an essential encounter that affirms humanity in a fresh way.

The festive sense here is that for a celebration of connection the drama is a great context. In it we gather our own depths and find a meaning that is a totally participatory one. The process is educational in the best sense: we learn by doing our dramatic depth work, we make a world in which others play important parts in our lives and we in theirs. The experience of being in a drama that has an archetypal or transpersonal basis is an expansive possibility that allows the imagination to leap into a creative kingdom that is both intimate and fictionally alive. The good festival allows a certain freedom to be enjoyed by everyone; in our workshops that freedom is at the heart of the work.

## 2

## TOWARDS A NEW DYNAMIC OF SOUL WORK

What is the goal of our work or of human work that enters the range of an art form? What is it to be inside the art, and not using the art for a moral or corrective purpose? There is a great deal of talk today of making people more functional, of getting in contact with the inner child, and the various nostrums that go along with co-dependency as a model for psychological truth. Blaming the previous generation seems to be at the heart of many of these considerations. And there is a dogmatism here, an identification with an extremely limited role in a generic story that is being told again and again. "I am an incest survivor." "I'm in recovery." "I was a sex addict," etc. etc. Again and again, those of us who work with people hear these broad categories of dilemma, positions they have accepted in their explicated worlds. But seldom does one hear the personal destiny or vital individuality that must be hidden in the person's life story. An idea, an abstraction, a tightly constructed diagnosis becomes the entire basis on which such a life teeters. But where is soul in all these mechanisms that dysfunction? Where is the individual? Many of these considerations are reductive and lack the wisdom to which we are actually heirs. In our workshops, when there is soulful energy that comes when there is a deep presenting issue with a reverberating silence underneath it, the entire group often senses the convergence of terrific layers of meaning that are figuratively unfolding to reveal a central order of reality, or a still point in the revolving world of our lives.

We make ritual, in our case, dramatic ritual, largely because we have lost rapport with soul either in the world or in our inner lives. Drama allows us to enter the ancient ritual of dialoguing with infinite expanses in a finite form. The universals return: Love dialogues with War, Old Age with Youth, Death with Birth, and there is a presentness to these bearers of universal news, a vivid ability to inhabit both dramatic intensities in our own time and space. The imaginative mind wants to experience transcendence because of the sense of freedom therein. And our work is grounded in the emancipation of perspective that has been granted all artists who pursue what Blake described as 'infinity in a grain of sand.' But our dramatic workers never attain an abstract state of perfection. We are seeking to enter, by way of imperfection of means, a dramatic world that has about it a freshness that comes from metaphor, the poetic use of the stage for the soul's movement.

We emphasize particulars, always. A place one visited. A dream image that calls forth the desire to rise in the world. The wind that kicked up on that walk by the sea. The splendid light at sunset in the desert.

**Do you see the bright sky and the dance of opposites? The thread of our work runs from the Greeks (and probably long before) into our present age that often seems teetering on some edge of infinite space. Will we make it? Will we make sense of this world and hand it on? So much has failed us. And yet the soul prevails, stands before the vastness of time. What is happening here, on the earth, in the pivotal dance that goes on and on? Do we need an ascensionist fantasy to pilot us into a benign future, that finds a new paradigm for comfort and glory? Or are we finding a way to ground ourselves in this condition, on this earth, with Death and the other archetypes to greet and console us? Is there a literal success we are seeking or is it rather more like an imaginal series of events that can be construed in a tremendous variety of ways? Are we ready for anything (as Rilke counseled the young poet) or are we trying to stake out a little piece of familiarity we can call our own, so that there is measure and finality and a limited sense of order. That larger expanse that takes us out of the familiar is perhaps more formidable, but also it just may be more human in the long run. We are the makers, the questioners and perhaps the inspired in whose souls the subtleties and complexities of history are being enacted.**

*

My thesis is that we are covering ground that was there all along, that there is a place for us that sends energy toward something new in the process of procuring from art something original and refreshing. Yes, there is technique in the work. That was the case all along. Acting coaches and therapy trainers line the streets of our major cities.

But our work is more than acting or therapy training. It is a challenge that goes deeply into theatre art but also stays within a possibility that what we do will consistently and spontaneously stir our depths, giving us a world to celebrate that is so much like our best possible courses of action that we feel we have reached some kind of apotheosis where education, therapy and theatre reach a confluence of intimate knowledge for each individual. And paradox is alive and well in our work, so that psychological complexity is the order of the day.

*

The theatre has always been a source of power for mankind and our groups sustain original theatrical impulse, pushing us further into the archetypal range of its dominant possibilities where we come close to our own truths, putting the psyche into a place that dances as it learns, shifting position to play new roles. The expansion that often occurs, the devotion to an expanded field of interest in which our concerns present themselves in concrete characters is a liberation of a kind that we can live with; it announces a world that parallels our own, giving the everyday an even deeper basis because it is coupled with another world. And in this way psychological or inner life is enriched, and we can meet the relationships of our ongoing life in new ways, because we have found our own innerness to be so full. The treasures of inner life can be shared and can build for each of us a storehouse that we can return to, no matter life's vicissitudes.

Jung is a help in our work. His body of work asks us to broaden perspectives to include material that has long been buried in human history. He is an excavator, an archaeologist of essential information for our human journey. He goes into the human record and finds in alchemy something we can all use: an amalgam of fruitful knowledge and speculative insight that has always been the soul of art.

What we are seeking in our work is archetypal experience. Like alchemists of old, we are searching for a language that ignites the imagination and at the same time sends us further into our own archetypal material. It is the idea of the archetypal basis of human wisdom that is part of the spur here. The alchemy we are seeking is based on a depth psychology that is no more bounded than the quests of spiritual man everywhere. We are employing the archetypal domain of man's psyche for the purpose of finding the larger truth of the human condition. We are not positing a secure spiritual standpoint; we are arguing that man's soul is part of the natural world and has specific needs that go beyond ego-consciousness. We have had signposts all along the way of our development, notions and moralities that have a certain validity. But we are again at an impasse: an upheaval of values is with us again, and the paradoxes of our intentions are often baffling. We seek a new condition, a new attitude to propel us toward transformations that will absorb this time and our destinies. And in our archetypal dramatic work, we have found a method of working that keeps a strong connection with the heart, with psychological truth, and with the archetypal root of our being. These are grounded in a universal force through whose agencies we find our own individual meaning.

## ℘ 3 ☙
## STAGING THE INTRODUCTION TO ARCHETYPAL DRAMA

*The ultimate fate of every dogma is that it gradually becomes soulless. Life wants to create new forms, and therefore, when a dogma loses its vitality, it must perforce activate the archetype that has always helped man to express the mystery of the soul.* (C.G. Jung, *Collected Works* 14, par. 488)

The director addresses the group: Hopefully, what we're going to be doing today is exploring several worlds: the inner world, both your own inner world and the larger inner world that Jung called the collective unconscious; as well as the world of archetypal drama which just could lead us back to the world itself, in all its natural profusion. We attempt to get back to the ancient ground of the theatre which always had at its root a ritual aspect that developed themes and characters around man's most relevant issues. The Greek theatre was a theatre dedicated to the god Dionysus, who was a god of poetry and energized celebration. Someone mentioned in a recent workshop that he felt that we might be back at the earliest and original impulses of the theatre. The archetype of the theatre, so to speak. The word archetype simply means 'first type' and implies an original form in the collective inherited knowledge of the species. In Jung's conception, the archetype possesses a dual nature: it's conscious and unconscious, symbolical and instinctive, psychic and non-psychic. The archetype is in a sense the hidden foundation of consciousness and the common origin of both behavioral and psychic events. Jung also said that the unconscious spontaneously personifies certain archetypal contents in dreams. And where Jung added certain mythological formulations to these personifications, we have found in archetypal drama that there are new ways of naming these entities that have to do with our own creative motifs and potentials.

Our idea here—which echoes Jung's "active imagination"—is that inner figures have an autonomy and vigor we can dialogue with and get to know as part of our inner worlds. We are going to be making drama and dialogue here today in a way that echoes the historical development of the drama. As an archetypal or first form, it seems to me that the drama was a way for earliest mankind to begin making sense of his or her often oppositional relationship to both nature and the spirit world. Jung talked about how many so-called primitive human groups have in their basic psychical operations the ability to dissociate, which means that they have many ways of relating to the world—sometimes trance states and various levels of unconscious and non-ego mental states. Dissociation, of course, in modern psychoanalytic practice, involves ideas about breaking apart and splitting. Mary Watkins and others have argued that a perspective that values dramatic experience would value multiplicity. In Multiple Personality Disorder (MPD) there is no imaginal dialogue, there is sequential monologue. MPD is often severe because one voice or alter takes over at any given time. Real dialogue with alters can often lead to real improvement in MPD.

The work that I propose is to allow the ego to have its status, but also bring in some of the phenomenal creative potential of archetypal realms where the dreams and the myths are born. Our work then becomes not merely cognitive, but imaginal and archetypal. Jung was well aware that the ego is an unsteady captain of the psychic ship. He also felt that what he called a "monotheism of consciousness" impoverishes the vast potential of the psyche. James Hillman and other post-Jungians talk about the heroic ego and want to give the imaginal underworld of the psyche a chance to live its own eventful existence without the ego's dominance. We'll talk more about this as we go on. In passing, though, we might say that dissociation, looked at in a certain way, is also part of how we come to understand parts of ourselves and begin to fathom the dimensions of our inner worlds that want a say in our own psychic process. In active imagination, Jung found that the ego could in fact dialogue with inner or unconscious figures. He termed this actively imaginative realm "psychoid," a sort of strange coining that was part of his brilliance as a creative thinker. Hillman uses the term "imaginal ego," something he says is capable of moving in the dark without literalizing dream or imaginative form. The emphasis is always on the imaginative construct, the de-literalized move.

In our work, the imagination is realized, as it is in poetry, art and theatre. The dramatic figures in our work have a specific energy that allows them to have a certain kind of being or existence. Participants are encouraged to ask questions or exercise your freedom to reject an action that feels to you like a wrong move. This kind of work is a way for you to take charge of your lives, to learn reflection in action, and to gather an independent vision. By using the inner musculature that creates dialogue with your own inner worlds, you gain a strength that can be life sustaining. Many of us have the habit of relying on others, on relationship, to be the sustenance of our lives. But our procedures introduce in a profound way the idea that you can enter into and present your own innerness. You can become a creator of your own dramas, and become friendly with an entire range of your own integrity. I see myself as mostly a helper or midwife for the dramas that are ready to come to life.

*

After our check-in where we have introductions, the early part of our work today will involve warming up. We don't begin any large-scale enactments without smaller movements. This is true in both theatre and dance as well. We slowly warm to the occasions of our larger purposes, and we first do simple exercises and then some small mini-dramas. I usually start with a mirroring exercise. Each participant chooses someone to work with, and one simply mirrors the other' s movements. We sometimes add vocal mirroring. Then we'll try some dialogues with two parts of your lives. In that exercise, I'll ask you to find two positions in your life—let's call them opposites—and we'll create a dramatic form out of that. A simple form of that would be the part that is a parent and the part that has a job in the world. There are many possibilities for warming up. We are getting ready for spontaneous dramatic unfolding.

Let me give you some sense of the procedure in which we will process an actual archetypal drama: We will first talk about the issues you want to deal with and then we will begin presenting the personified ideas and then you will cast them from the group. These will be the auxiliaries or helpers who will engage you in essential dialogue. We will then move toward the enactment itself. By this time, fully in the swing of the work, the heart of the creative process should be underway. You as the protagonist will most likely role-reverse with the other characters. There will often be additional characters cast as we go along. Most of you will be accompanied throughout the piece by a companion chosen from the group.The companion can play roles or serve as an inner guide or as a consultant in your unfolding process. At the end of the major portion of the enactment, we usually have a closing moment and then we ask you to de-role everyone who has been cast. And finally, we have an open-ended group sharing in which all of us acknowledge the effect your work had on us, what it meant and how your work resonated with experiences we have had. What we are doing here has parallels in the studio-based approach to art therapy: we are taking you into the heart of the drama itself and the self-discovery we are seeking emerges from the art itself.

We deal with ways of telling stories, our own ways of making dialogue. The healing potential I think comes when we recognize our own lives as ongoing creative enterprises. We have access to ways of looking forward and backward, and ways to create new and changed forms of experience. And the roles we enact will hopefully provide us with a charged sense of significance—that our lives can in fact form a dramatic action that has definition and place and purpose. We attempt to expand the dramatic imagination toward new possibilities of experience and interest in life. Some of us may even enter the archetype of the hero, stretching our ability to work at the edge of our human capacity.

## 4
## POLAR OPPOSITES IN ARCHETYPAL DRAMA

*Clear-cut distinctions and strict formulations are quite impossible in this field, seeing that a kind of fluid interpenetration belongs to the very nature of all archetypes.* (CW 9, 1, par. 301)

Our work is grounded in paradox and ambivalence. We seek psychic wholeness and psychic polarities are the stuff out of which that completeness is reached. Our work has definite resonance with analytical psychology in this regard. Jung's entire body of work is replete with opposites: conscious and unconscious; enantiodromia in which one polarity of an opposition reverses into its opposite; psychological functions which include oppositional attitudes (introversion/extroversion) which occur in polar pairs; recurrent archetypal polarities such as logos and eros, power and love, ego and shadow, and, late in his career in his alchemical studies, the male-female polarity and the *coniunctio* became major concerns. In our work we learn this tension of opposites and its possible answers to age old questions. There is a dramatic dialectic that is very old in theatre history. In this tension of polarities, there is the potential for great expressive energy. A good example of this is this exchange between Iago and Othello in Shakespeare's *Othello:*

IAGO. Good name in man and woman, dear my lord,
Is the immediate jewel of their souls.
Who steals my purse steals trash; 'tis something, nothing;
'Twas mine, 'tis his, and has been slave to thousands;
But he that filches from me my good name
Robs me of that which not enriches him,
And makes me poor indeed.
OTHELLO. By heaven, I'll know thy thoughts.
IAGO. You cannot, if my heart were in your hand,
Nor shall not, whilst 'tis in my custody.
OTH. Ha?
IAGO. O, beware, my lord, of jealousy!
It is the green eyed monster which doth mock
The meat it feeds on. That cuckold lives in bliss
Who, certain of his fate, loves not his wronger;
But O, what damnèd minutes tells he o'er
Who dotes, yet doubts; suspects, yet strongly loves!
OTH. O misery!
IAGO. Poor and content is rich, and rich enough,
But riches fineless is as poor as winter

To him that ever fears that he will be poor.
Good God, the souls of all my tribe defend
From jealousy!
OTH. Why? Why is this?
Think'st thou I'd make a life of jealousy?
To follow still the changes of the moon
With fresh suspicions? No! To be once in doubt
Is once to be resolved.... (III, iii, 155-180)

Iago is supplying the oppositional force to all that Othello stands for. He is becoming the impediment to his peace, his love, his very existence. They are becoming severely polarized, even as Othello is ironically able to say "This fellow's of exceeding honesty/ And knows all qualities with a learned spirit...."

In this situation, Iago is playing a numinous shadow figure, and Othello's fascination with his qualities is corrupting all his capacity for reason and discernment. These opposing forces make up this tragedy, and the redeeming wisdom Othello so desperately needs is missing altogether.

In our work, we learn this tension of opposites and its possible answers to age old questions through dialogue. The ambivalence becomes two players in a staged operation involving puer/senex, high/low, male/female, love/hate. The dialectic poses the question and finds answers in opposition. This is the conjunction in which we are containing the polarities, in which we are at the heart of archetypal knowing. Here are examples of this kind of process:

Ego-Driven. I stand for what's real in the world. I want to control the world's material goods. Nothing can stop me. I own homes, I have bank accounts, I do not like to think in abstractions. I am a veritable emperor. I have fourteen cars, three houses, and an office that works like a clock.

Soul-Centered. I'm another part of the world. I am deep in the mystery of existence, and I find the world active and alert. I live in another dimension. I am what grounds existence in the depths of life. I connect you with beauty and poetry and the realms that give meaning even in the midst of uncertainty.

Or:

Isolation: I need to be free from all contact with others. I cannot find truth without this complete distancing from the other.

Togetherness: I need the satisfaction of being with others. It is a testimony to my energy that I attract others.

Isolation. You scare me. I do not like closeness. I'm shy.

Togetherness: There you can rely on me. I will show the inner truth of a closeness.

And so on. Archetypal consciousness is achieved through paradoxical experience. We learn to tolerate the in-between, we become integrated *in* the opposing movements of the split archetypal forces. It is no simple task. It requires a surrender to psychic wounding, for the ego would have us take sides in all this. The ego would secure us in the singleness of a vision that would make us heroic. We must take another stand if we are to achieve the completeness of the archetypal quest. What we are after is enduring the tension of opposites in order to achieve what Jung called the 'transcendent function of opposites.'

We have in the West a long tradition of seeking spiritual heights. As Jung (1959) remarked: "The West is always seeking uplift, but the East seeks a sinking or deepening." In our work we always have an eye toward compensatory activity, that recurring theme in which archetypal energy is reunited with its polar opposite.

*In our check-in at the group's beginning, Jane mentioned that she was terror-struck lately by the prospect of her 22 year old son going to prison for drugs and other problems. She also stated that she had been sexually abused when young and that this also entered into her fears for her son. The original positions she created were Brutality and Terror, in opposition, with a character called The Web encircling them. After spurts of this configuration, she decided to dissolve this and moved on to something else. This involved creating pairings with her son at various ages: 2 years, 9 years and 17 years. In each case she created a character representing herself juxtaposed/opposite the son. At first, a merging mother, then a mother leaving her very angry 9 year old, then facing him at 17 with acknowledgment that his attitudes and acting out came from her leaving him. We then moved into the present and she dialogued with him about their mutual need to resolve this together, with her asking him to come live with her. There was a deep rapproachment and a generosity that seemed to have a real basis in her feeling about the situation. The sharing concerned different points of view on children, especially the issue of divorce as it applies to children.*

This piece was not traditionally oppositional. But it had about it two opposing points of view, one in which the awful repercussions of drugs and the legal system bore down on her sense of what might befall her son. The shifted position involved elements of caring and love and concern coupled with the anger that was generated when she left him. These were, in a sense, oppositional, yet slightly removed from the usual oppositions that involve polarities like love/hate or interior/exterior. The possibility of terror and abuse still exists, but Jane went inside of her problem in the later phase, deepening her knowledge of the problem and its historical antecedents. Love as a force to compensate for these earlier problems also entered the mix.

A more typical opposition might occur between Eros and Logos. This might proceed something like this:

Eros. I'm the momentum of your love life. I attract all kinds of objects and I run with it. I'm the heart of the thrilling empire of desire. I'm nurturant and free, I'm eternally alive to pleasure. I was what spurred your earlier life and you lived at a time when I could go wild. You thought I was going to keep your life full of meaning, but times have changed. I am no longer the innocent sacred substance born of your desire to rebel. But I still pack potency, I am still capable of taking you over.

Logos. I'm meaning and thought. I am the words that come to you to make certain that there is understanding in the world. I give countenance to your best and most poignant mental ability. I lead you to wisdom that contains Apollonian structure.

Eros. I'm not interested in intellect at all. I want to dance in the delight of the body. I want Dionysus to introduce me to sensual mystery. I love the sight and song of the dance! I want my energy to create enthusiastic experience!

Logos. I define the universe. For me there is the splendid shape of a fine thought, the deep meaning of expression and the thoughtfulness of life. There is a moral surety in me which is not found when the passions are intense. I offer repose, serenity and a surrender to pleasures that stir in the mind.

Another way of construing this would be the head and the heart, or Dionysus and Apollo. The opposites create a dialogical whole and they give the psyche a place to reach new levels of wholeness. It is an exercise in active imagination as well, and brings the imagination of the two elements into a relevant conjunction. As Jung has written:

> Ascent and descent, above and below, up and down, represent an emotional realization of opposites, and this realization leads, or else should lead, to their equilibrium.... As Dorn interprets it, this vacillating between the opposites and being tossed back and forth means being contained *in* the opposites. They become a vessel in which what was previously now one thing and now another floats vibrating, so that the painful suspension between opposites gradually changes into the bilateral activity of the point in the centre. (CW 14, par. 296)

In our dramatic construction this in-between or center-space becomes part of the work that aims at liberation from either polarity. We are looking for a widening of consciousness or a greater experience of wholeness. And so the work has its parallels with the individuation process in that it explores the forward movement of the knowledge of opposites with the idea of a conjunction that transcends the polarities. In this way, we sometimes create a mediating position between two opposites, so that the psychological worker can see both sides from a central perspective. We sometimes call this character The Bridge or The Mediator. Here is an example of how this works:

Acceptance. I accept this condition entirely. I will abide by the rules of your school and I will learn what you want me to learn.

Judgment. This is not acceptable. This is a thoroughly trashed and insane reality. I do not want to be part of a school that makes me feel defined by someone else's rules.

Bridge. I'm the bridge between these worlds. It's important for you to finish your work here. I will take what's good in this, and disregard what is not useful to me. But I will reconcile the two positions because neither one of you has the whole truth. I want you to find a way to continue with this work, neither accepting wholesale everything the school stands for, nor judging it worthless and running away. There is something to learn here, something to complete. Trust me.

So the work has many motions, but its insistence is on allowing distinct energies from each position to enact their full potential while permitting a reconciliation or a transcendence if this is possible. Sometimes, we find that the positions are entrenched and there is no mediation between the opposing energies. But generally there is an inclination for some kind of rapport, or at least an honoring of the polarized positions.

## ꧁ 5 ꧂
## ARCHETYPAL DREAM DIALOGUES

*In the theatre of the future there will be no spectators. People will act for themselves, without audiences and actors, by themselves.* (Leonid Andreyev)

Freud's dream method involved free-association or dissolving the dream back into the dreamer's personal past. Jung's amplification, moving in another direction, takes the imaginal elements and gives them a dialogical home in the working metaphorical/mythical capacity of the dreamer. The world of the archetypal or collective contents can then enter the life of the dreamer, creating a dialogic potential that is quite broad. Sometimes, the dialogue becomes an occasion for a fictive adventure that enters another realm or *terra incognita*. As an example, I had a dream with a huge shaft of gold-yellow light rising like a pillar, with a reclining male dream figure at the bottom of it. I later created a dialogue that went like this:

—What are you?
—A shaft of golden energy.
—What do you want?
—I am what I want. I am that blissful golden light that incessantly rises beyond the merely human and earthly.
—What are you in the dream?
—To remind you of that splendid curiosity we call Eternal Delight.
—Which is what?
—Colossal, vibrant, whole, immortal Energy. I exist.
—What can I learn from you?
—The world beyond is within. That I am there inside. That the beauty that contains this light is a part of eternity and is a part of you.
—Can I do anything to keep you active?
—Seeing and no more. That is the task here. Seeing.

And the reclining male figure dialogued as follows:

—Reclining figure, what are you?
—I slumber at the foot of the light. But I am part of the effort.
—Why do you sleep?
—In order to fulfill the dream. There is essence in the dream.
—Yes. But will you wake?
—My task is to dream. The light is born of the dream.
—How can I work with you, give you room to stay in the dream?
—We do what we can. I must dream.

So that personal history is somehow bypassed in order to find the imaginative context for the next step in the work. And this has echoes in the alchemical operations Jung was so fond of. The conscious worker or dream ego gets to create a metaphorical occasion in which the dream's raw material is transformed into yet another entity—a dialogue, a drama, a play of forces conscious and unconscious. The dream lends itself to this kind of effort because its intrinsic existence is already part of a separate reality, the night world with its unpredictable capacity for epiphany and undiscovered imaginative form.

The archetypal dream staging allows a certain movement to occur. We usually have the person present all the dream figures from the first person perspective. Then we cast the figures and begin dialoguing and proceeding with the dream sequence. Sometimes, in the presentation of a dream figure, there is a great deal of affect generated and the person has a sudden realization of the dream's deeper purpose. The dreamer will often present a conscious situation that has some relevance to the dream, so that we can see the parallel worlds of the conscious and unconscious positions.

In staging a dream, we want to keep the integrity of the dream intact while allowing a movement in and out of conscious reality. It's important to remember that the dream worker is conscious while presenting the dream, but the drama allows a movement back into the unconscious figures of the dream world. Sometimes, it becomes clear that the dream material has awakened a conscious struggle in the worker and so we must deal with that, allowing the day world issues to come forth. The director must be sensitive here to the dream's integrity, which often holds archetypal motifs unbeknownst to the dream worker.

Here's a dream of mine with a central image: *In the dream I catch a great salmon, which my friend Peter helps to bring in. I watch the whole beautiful salmon on the dock, becoming aware that in order to harvest it, it will have to die.*

Here's my active imagination dialogue with the salmon:

Bill. What are you, oh salmon?
Salmon. Your fish.
B. What does it mean to you, to be caught in your wholeness?
S. I am simply perfect, though I must die.
B. I see that. What does your existence mean?
S. I come from the deeps and I am beautiful.
B. I must eat you.
S. You will, yes. But first you must harvest me.
B. What does harvest mean?
S. To complete the transformation.
B. Of what?
S. Of your innerness, your beauty, your soul.

B. So your appearance in this dream is metaphorical?
S. Yes.
B. For what?
S. Completeness. It is time.
B. And what is my first task?
S. You must bring me in. You must stop my cycle of return and bring me to rest.
B. Rest?
S. From my constant cycle of return.

From this I gathered the need to stop a certain pattern of returning to origin to recreate the circumstances of my early experience. I tend to repeat the original experience, to find my way back to the child's original conditions with the mother. In my conscious amplification of the dream content, I imagine the dream is giving me a vision of individuation that has to do with stopping the cycle, of entering the process at another level. The return need not continue. It is time to harvest a wholeness. It is time for completion of the soul work.

Hillman (1979) is insistent that the dream "is not mine, but the psyche's." Thus we go into the dream's darkness not to elucidate the night world for the sake of the waking ego, but to learn the soul's territory, to teach the ego how to enter the metaphorical ground of the underworld.

> The imaginal ego is at home in the dark, moving among images as one of them...That the dream is like a shadow play, a mask, further connects it with the underworld...The Dionysian aspect of Hades does indeed make the dream akin to the drama, as Jung said...In the drama of our dreams you and I, even if we are in the audience, are in the theatre, actors all of us, dream-persons all of us, wearing the mask appropriate for the character we must play in the way we must play it. (pp. 102-103).

This sense of play is pivotal in my thesis throughout this work. I want to turn now to another one of my dreams, one with a theatrical context and see where it leads in this discussion. I'll write it out in its original shorthand.

**Arthur Miller (the playwright) in the dream. I ask him if anyone wanted to do *After The Fall* as a film. (1964 play starring Jason Robards with a character, Maggie, resembling Marilyn Monroe). He says no.**

**I'm in Joe's cabin. I escape out the back way when assault by big film crew comes. I hide out.**

**I jump very high. I hover in the air. I think I can make this work for basketball, but my timing is not right.**

**A woman takes my keys. She returns them, but keeps keys that belong to another woman's house.**

**I'm in a play directed by a woman at a college. She gives everyone parts but me. She tells me I had to make arrangements to have a part. I tell her she did not want me in the play. I decide to quit the school.**

**I call two friends in the east to see if they want to go on a long bike ride. They say it will be too cold in Canada. They say it will be better out west. I haven't decided what to do.**

So, depending on our perspective, we have the dream's workings. Is there a message here, a Jungian compensation? A Freudian wish-fulfillment? Are we dealing with a psychological problem here or is the challenge cultural and artistic, alchemical and underworld? What was at work in the dream? From the day world we could include a writer's concerns (with an admired author), escape from view (the hideout), puer (eternal boy) flight and visions of stardom in 'high' sporting behavior (basketball and jumping); the kept key and the authority and wisdom therein, perhaps of Sophia; the anima woman directing the play who says I have to make arrangements and whose call to action I answer by quitting (calling off the relation to anima); and the persistent indecisiveness of the final section about the long ride somewhere.

But what else is going on here? What desire is being fulfilled in the dream images, the dream staging? Hillman reminds us that "for both Freud and Jung the work that goes on in sleep fulfills an instinctual or archetypal need.... In some amazing way, instinct is satisfied in the night world by its own images, images of itself, as if it were enough for the psyche to see its own reflection by means of images, as if it were enough to imagine in poetic form its physical body and needs, its love, and its own self." (1979, p. 121) So the dream becomes a living reflection of the imaginal reality of the psyche. In Hillman's view, rather than the (ego's) labors of Hercules, we get the (psyche's) reflections of Narcissus, leaving the imaginative ambiguity to do its own work.

For purposes of archetypal drama, let us take a section of this dream and imagine a conversation between the dream's Arthur Miller and the dream-ego's questioner. (A.M. & D.E.)

A.M. What do you want?

D.E. I've been thinking I'd like to make a film of *After the Fall*. I've always been fascinated by it. I think it says so much. It seems to all take place in Quentin's mind, and I was always amazed by how much is going on there. Quentin is overwhelmed by his past. He wants to know if he should marry again. He wants to know about the war and the world of suffering.

A.M. You want to be a writer.

D.E. Well, yes, I do, I think writing is a great activity. And you have done so much important writing. I see you as writing about the American archetypal world, about the undercurrents in the American psyche. I think Willy Loman (*Death of a Salesman*) is quintessential archetypal stuff.

A.M. What are you writing?

D.E. I want to write about the world of my own dreams. I keep having anima attacks. I don't know if I'm dreaming all this or if I actually have a life. Sometimes, I imagine I'm going through all these stages and trials, but in reality it's going on in some kind of dream state. What can you teach me?

A.M. It takes time. You have to play with your own depth. Each thing is made again. You have terrible experiences, losses, death, but you put it back into the mix, the alchemy of the work. You keep at it, or you give up. You have your own story to tell. Get with it.

D.E. There is this great unknown in me. I want to live it out, I feel I can and yet it doesn't seem to materialize. I know the stuff is there. I need the guts to go ahead and work on all this.

Arthur Miller is here seen as the heroic archetypal writer, the keen knower of things denied to the Dream Ego. Or there is a confluence of possible energy here and there is knowledge of forces that have not yet congealed. Things are in flux. Arthur Miller stands as an exemplar of this inner process of transformation. But there is a lack of nerve in the dream's ways and means. From the dream: One can suspect puer (boyish) dynamics in the jumping in the air, but the timing is not right. The anima woman takes the keys. There is a conflict over the part in the play. Arrangements need to be made. I quit the school, begin the old traveling gambit again. Escape artistry rather than digging into the work. There is perhaps some kind of trickster here, something screwing up the works. No decision. Where to hide? What to do with the keys. Hiding out, bad timing, keys to another's house, a play not consummated, the incomplete ride. One can foresee trouble here, a lack of connection while the world advanced as a possibility here is represented by the inner work so prominent in Miller's play: Quentin, confused and disturbed by life, by his life and the lives of those around him (including the great Aphroditic Maggie), still keeps trying to find his way in the great maze of modernity. Of course the play wasn't made into a film. The play was a box office failure (despite Robards) and did not get much critical acclaim either. Miller was also chastised for bringing his problems with Marilyn Monroe so graphically to the stage.

So the dream has about it some failed connections and projects that really don't go anywhere. There is the hopeful connection with turning this kind of world into literary creation; there are also troubling aspects here, of quitting and running away, of losing threads that might lead to decision.

*

*The soul desires to dwell with the body because without the members of the body it can neither act nor feel.* (Leonardo da Vinci)

In archetypal drama, we move the soul-work back to the body, and include it in our imaginal activity. It is true enough that the dream occurs beyond the body, in some kind of image-realm, but it is our purpose to bring the entire world of the actor's repertory into our work. The voice is important, and the face, the hands and torso. For us the archetypal images and figures are translated spontaneously into physical action. Michael Chekhov (1953) has developed ideas on what he calls the psychological gesture:

> There are two kinds of gestures. One we use both while acting on the stage and in everyday life—the natural and usual gesture. The other kind is what might be called the archetypal gesture, one which serves as an original model for all possible gestures of the same kind. (p. 66)

The gesture serves a sort of cue, a stirring of deeper forces, and it calls us into 'the soup' of the inner work, to the great churning of inner resources. It is a way to open the gates to creative work, to fulfilling the project at hand, the revelation of human personality.

The Polish director Jerzy Grotowski takes Chekhov's views even further. He talks about the 'total act of the actor:'

> It is the act of laying oneself bare, of tearing off the mask of daily life, of exteriorizing oneself. Not in order to show oneself off, for that would be exhibitionism. It is a serious and solemn act of revelation. The actor must be ready to be absolutely sincere. It is like a step toward the summit of the actor's organism in which are united consciousness and instinct. (Cole, 1970, p. 533)

And the conditions for this require that the actor work 'in security': "An atmosphere must be created, a working system in which the actor feels that he can do absolutely anything, that nothing he does will be the object of jokes, that all will be understood and accepted." (Ibid., p. 533)

The creation of an atmosphere in which work can emerge from its dormant state is a theme that runs through much theatre work and occurs just as often in our dramatic therapy work. It is not about self-aggrandizement or stardom; it is about "an act of extreme yet disciplined sincerity and authenticity." (Ibid., p. 534) Grotowski's quest was to find in the revelatory acting of others the heart of his work:

> I was first trained as an actor, then as a director.... Little by little I developed and discovered that to fulfill myself was far less fruitful than studying the possibility for self-realization in others.... If I can attain from the actor—in collaboration with him—a total self-revelation, as with Ryszard Cieslak in *The Constant Prince*, this is for me far more fertile than putting together once again, or that is to say, to create purely in my own name. Little by little, I have, therefore, oriented myself towards parascientific research in the field of the actor's art. (Ibid., p. 535)

As for aims that go beyond the merely psychological, archetypal drama follows Hillman's line of reasoning apropos dreaming:

> The phenomenon to be saved is the dream, saved from its day world links, which distort the images in personal recollections. Our anamnesis is the dream itself, and we get to know the patient through his dreams, from below, turning to his psyche before his day world life. This move constellates the underworld from the beginning and initiates the whole analytical procedure as a descent into unknown space. (1979, p. 196)

The dream is not personal history, though there are elements of history in its formal presentation. As Ernst Cassirer (1944) comments: "What a drama gives us, Aristotle asserts, is a single action which is a complete whole in itself, with all the organic unity of a living creature; (Art) does not inquire into the qualities or causes of things; it gives us the intuition of the form of things.... It is a true and genuine discovery. The artist is just as much a discoverer of the forms of nature as the scientist is a discoverer of facts or natural laws." (pp. 143-44)

The drama, like the dream, discloses an inner content that is revealing of the depth of human process. Cassirer, again:

> Shakespeare never gives us an aesthetic theory. He does not speculate about the nature of art. Yet in the only passage in which he speaks of the character and function of dramatic art the whole stress is laid upon the aliveness and immediacy of emotion: "The purpose of playing," as Hamlet explains, "both at the first and now, was and is, to hold, as 'twere, the mirror up to nature; to show virtue her own feature, scorn her own image, and the very age and body of the time his form and pressure." (Ibid., pp. 147-48)

Like the drama, the dream tells its own story and gives its inner events their own significance. There has been much interest (in dramatic theory as well as in psychodrama) in the question of catharsis, as originally promoted by Aristotle. Cassirer re-visions the issues and offers a new clarity:

> The cathartic process described by Aristotle does not mean a purification or a change in the character and quality of the passions themselves but a change in the human soul. By tragic poetry the soul acquires a new attitude toward its emotions. The soul experiences the emotions of pity and fear, but instead of being disturbed and disquieted by them it is brought to a state of rest and peace.... (Ibid., p. 148)

*

I often have students choose an historical character with whom they would like to have a dialogue. This permits a deep dramatic meditation on the life of an historical personage with whom one is often surprisingly very familiar. It's usually very revealing and charges the atmosphere with imaginal possibility. Some of the ones I remember include Amelia Earhart, Harry Truman, Eleanor Roosevelt, the Biblical David, St. Paul and St. Francis of Assisi. Here is one with the poet Rainer Maria Rilke (1874-1926):

## CONVERSATION WITH RILKE

—Rene, I've often wondered how you were able to write your great poems. It seems like you were always seeking privacy and distance from people.

—The poetry came first. I had only so much energy. People use up energy.

—What was it like at Duino Castle when you were working on the Elegies? Wasn't it too spacious for one person?

—I needed the space to find room for those co-conspirators of my creative process, the angels, who were accompanying me on the journey. Space was essential.

—How consciously did you work on the Elegies?

—I had to be alert. Sometimes, sleep was impossible. But I must say they were largely given to me. I was the receiver of inspiration. The words came to me, as if by grace.

—How do you feel about having given up family, children and those regular human occurrences to pursue your work?

—My work was my life. In it I was a power. It was what I was meant to do. I felt it as a calling. So the cost was never important. I did what I had to do.

—I'm amazed & overwhelmed by the quality of so much of your work, especially *The Sonnets to Orpheus* and *The Duino Elegies*. Can you give me some sense of how you feel about poetry now?

—It feels less grand than in my time. In my time, we still had ideas of artistic vision that come from another order of reality, a kind of spiritual certainty. Disillusionment was strong after The First War, but you have seen a bitter turn against the spirit of exaltation I fought for. You must go further to find the means in which to discover everlasting praise. But it's there and you can find it within you and I'm glad the attempt is still there. Be willing to go inward. It is no small cause and the strains of hopeful music there engendered can fill a small gymnasium. The calling is ever to celebrate renewal with the voices of praise. Life is difficult, as is death. But there is great meaning in all our transitoriness. To be awake to expressions of our lives is the task of the poet, who must rise and sing of the heart of things.

## 6
## TRIBAL DREAMS

*The theatre is a house of dreams, in which audiences gather to share a dream that is presented to them by a group of artists who are particularly skilled in bodying forth dreams.... A fine performance...is also a highly sophisticated version of that experience...where members of the tribe gather together to be told a great dream which is of importance to the tribe. (Jung and the Theatre,* Robertson Davies)

As an actor, I have often been struck by the almost dreamlike condition that occurs in the course of acting in a play. There is in the concentration and intensity of the acting experience something defiant of ordinary consciousness. One feels oneself at a depth that rediscovers the power and beauty of psycho-physical events that create new energy and new ideas. As Adam and Alee Blatner (1988) put it in *The Art of Play*, "what psychoanalysis has discovered is the pervasiveness of mental phenomena which not only resist definition, but actively defy it, flout it, and subtly celebrate the poetry of the wisdom and beauty embedded in transrational states of consciousness.... The vehicle of dramatic play offers a method for bringing consciousness and social validation to the forces of imagery." (p. 165)

In order to give you a glimpse of my own creative concerns as an actor-director, I'd like to digress a bit and talk about performances. My favorite experiences in the theatre have involved a sense of being transported, of being in the presence of real magic. In 1965, I saw Morris Carnovsky's *King Lear*, at the Pilgrimage Playhouse in Los Angeles. That was a towering performance and I felt the power of the play in a way that has rarely happened since, though Olivier's performances (on film) of *Othello* and his late version of *King Lear* were for me amazing in another way. Peter Brook's nine hour saga *The Mahabharata* (based on the epic poem from India) closed in on archetypal themes that seemed wonderfully alive to me. The international cast was excellent and I found the staging terrific and potent and wildly archetypal—with tons of reddish earth and the Ganges running upstage, plus the use of fire and the sense of truly ancient sound and action (helped by the assortment of musical instruments and the scenic design). The piece generated a kind of return to the basic primal metaphors of human action: birth, family, war, death and renewal. It was an exhaustingly splendid occasion. I have also found performances by the Wooster Group that involved multi-media explorations to be wondrous in our tradition of rich tribal dreams partaking of archetypal themes.

Hillman (1983) in *Healing Fiction* speaks of 'daimon' and 'unconscious' as modes of imagining, modes of writing fictions, and both have their healing efficacy as the case may be. Imagination goes on in the commonplace and everyday 'unimaginative' language. And quoting Jung: "The great advantage of... 'daimon' and 'God' lies in making possible a much better objectification of the vis a vis, namely, a personification of it. The emotional quality confers life and effectuality upon them. Hate and love, fear and reverence, enter the scene of the confrontation and raise it to a drama. What has merely been 'displayed' becomes 'acted.'" (CW 5, par. 388)

The dramatic interchange recurs as perhaps the most potent way to present imaginative material. For it is the action between personified elements that creates the energy that rises to new occasions, allowing emotion to enter the work in a powerful way. Just as Hamlet was able to get information from his father's ghost, so the dramatic work in archetypal drama also derives its unique power from constantly digging into particular and universal, my father and Father as archetype. And these entities have their own voices, their own emotional energy, and allow us to enter their imaginal, objective existences. The parallel with Jung's 'active imagination' is not to be missed. And the demands are often similar: "So it is no wonder that the details of a transformation process rendered visible through active imagination make no small demands on our understanding." *(Archetypes,* CW 9, 1, par. 621) This is where knowledge of the theatrical entities we call into play can allow a certain assimilation into consciousness, thus rendering the emotional impact of the archetypal experience useful to the understanding of their contents. In the following active imagination, the two forces, Ego and Anima, engage in a dialogue about the nature of relationship:

*

## EGO (B) & ANIMA (A)

B. What do you want?
A. To be as I am.
B. You need a place to stay?
A. Always, and with you. You are mine.
B. What can I do to help?
A. Open me to you, as ever.
B. I'd like us to do important things together, but I don't quite know how.
A. It just needs time and place. We can go on a romp, we can talk and play.
B. Just like real couples do?
A. We are real enough.
B. But I can't hold your hand.
A. But you can hold my heart.
B. How?
A. Press close, and rejoin.
B. But that feels different from another person.
A. Oh, yes, no doubt.

B. But for you it's not enough?
A. It's enough.
B. But what about the quest for a mate.
A. It comes and goes, you belong to me.
B. So there is no finding an actual mate?
A. I can't say. There is much to be said about that.
B. I look and look. You can be with me.
A. Yes.

Here an important life-lesson about the nature of inner experience has occurred. The ego is aware that the quest for a real person is different from the experience with an inner figure. The anima becomes a guide to an experience different from the quest for a mate. She is an archetypal figure who desires to be known on her own terms.

*The theater, insofar as people are serious in it, seems to be looking for a place where it is not a duplication of life.... Most of the creative work is done in dream life, and this sometimes requires that the actor rest, and let the image move itself.... There are zones in us which know more than we think they do. The secret is knowing how to listen to them.* (Joseph Chaiken, 1972, pp. 25-6)

My students at Prescott College often present a marvelous ability to move from the personal to the archetypal and be at home in either realm. They want to explore, they *do* explore and the group is all the better for their exuberance and playful depth. Without real courage that makes the heart dig into the soul's deep emotional life there would be no yield. In the following drama, a male student brought to our group a burning desire to stay with one theme, *sexuality*, and take it as far as we could imagine it:

*John's subject was sexuality and it had been a problem for some time. He first cast Venus and reversed roles with her and gave her the prismatic sense of female sexuality that was transcendent. He then cast a male figure which he called Cthonic Male Sexuality and it was in the mood to make love: it humped and grinded across the stage. We then discussed everywoman and first cast everywoman as a manhater, a grudging kind of force that had been violated by men; we added her sister-opposite, the lover of male sexuality that comes from the sweeter side of the coin. Mention was made of the protagonist's mother, and we brought her out. She said she had taken him to Planned Parenthood and that he knew what he needed to know about sex. He remembered his mother scolding him for playing 'doctor' when he was very young and we reenacted that scene. He asked mother why there was so much sexual repression between her and his father. She had no reply. We then cast both The Great Mother and The Great Father.... The Great Mother said she supported him and wanted him to feel her power. The Great Father kissed Cthonic Male Sexuality and said he was always there, ready to rise to whatever occasion to help him. He went back to his inner world. The director suggested Eros as the final player for the occasion and the protagonist cast the last remaining member of the group to play Eros, and she, forever young, led him on a happy dance around the newly created world of his archetypal and personal journey through sexuality.*

*

In some way, the workshop itself becomes a kind of tribal dream. The work enters its own space, as theatre experience always has. There is perhaps slumbering in each of us the energy to act, to create an atmosphere where we are viewed by others in our most secret (and sacred) state. In the dream atmosphere of the drama, we enact our passionate concerns. We transgress boundaries, we go ahead with long abandoned plans. Our task becomes one in which we are sharing a depth with others, giving it a place to live. It is of importance to all because the group is there to find the supports each person needs to formalize the theme, to give breath to the dramatic entanglement.

## ℘ 7 ℘
# STANISLAVSKY, MORENO AND A JUNGIAN CODA

*The hours an actor spends in the theatre at rehearsals must gradually lead to his transformation into a full man—a man who is a creator in art, the sort of fighter for beauty and love who would be able to transfuse into the hearts of his listeners the whole meaning of each word and sound he utters on stage.... The actor is the force that reflects all the mysteries of nature....* (Konstantin Stanislavsky)

> His (Stanislavsky's) actor, because of working in two dimensions, develops a warming up process which is abortive and embryonic along spontaneous lines to be obliterated later on—and another warming up process, organized and conserved, which is to absorb and translate the inspirations received from what we psychodramatists call spontaneous states into conserved and uncreative phrasing, that is, uncreated by the actor. (Jacob Moreno)

Here we have differing views of the creative process involved in acting (and psychodrama) from two major figures in our study of the relationship between theatre work and truth. Stanislavsky, the director of art theatre, and Moreno, the director of therapeutic theatre, stand at radically different points on our discursive stage. Stanislavsky's "The actor is the force that reflects all the mysteries of nature" has about it an archetypal grandeur in which the actor reveals something of the infinite to those souls who don't have the talent to enter those realms of 'beauty and love.' Moreno, on the other hand, insists on the creative act being the work of the individual who is creating in the moment, freed from the demands of the 'cultural conserve' or the authority of the text which the actor must serve in order to perform a scripted work. Moreno is arguing for a kind of creative purity, "the act of creation contemporaneous with the production," so that "Spontaneity Training leads to a form of learning which aims at a greater unity and energy of personality.... The primary objective is the training in spontaneous states and not the learning of contents. Emphasis upon contents results in the split of the individual into an act personality and a content personality." (*Psychodrama*, pp. 138-9)

Stanislavsky, on the other hand, was interested in art in some traditional European sense, with great texts as the springboards for the actor's art. Stanislavsky used the term 'creative circle' to describe a condition in which the actor has the sense that he is performing in 'public solitude.'

> What is a 'circle?' It is that degree of concentration on one single thought in which all the nerves through which attention carries on its work are brought into focus.... They must also be tied together by the

> exercise of the utmost alertness of mind, so that they should all be working in the same direction.... (Stanislavsky, p. 145)

Stanislavsky advocates a kind of self-renunciation in which the 'personal life' of the actor is left behind, so that the creative imagination can find the proper 'repose' to enter the creative circle:

> The first thing an actor must do on entering the rehearsal room is to shed all the ties that bind him to his private life.... And the man who is sitting there now is the man whose part the actor has come to rehearse. A feeling of great calm must fill his heart.... Here, in this 'now,' there exists no other life than his creative life; here is only the powerful life of his spirit which enables him, through concentration, attention, mental alertness and self-renunciation, to transform himself into the character of the play.... (Ibid., pp. 150-51)

Interestingly, both Stanislavsky and Moreno seem deeply concerned with the sacred aspect of this work, the importance of creative activity, its intrinsic meaning and methods to ensure a complete experience. But Moreno's emphasis is on the therapeutic potential for the individual entering the spontaneous drama while Stanislavsky is deeply interested in "those hundreds of thousands of men and women whom [the actor's] creative work must influence by the power of beauty." (Ibid., p. 155) What often occurs among those unfamiliar with the spontaneous theatre is that there is a prejudice against instant, unscripted, unrehearsed drama. But those of us who have been involved in dramatic enactment that unfolds from the soul's instantaneous immersion in its own action-formation know by heart experiences that went far beyond anything that could be called slipshod or unrehearsed. It's as if the ensemble in the instant archetypal theatre knows from some ancient historical memory exactly how to set and stage the most complex inner events.

Moreno is on a different track from Stanislavsky, in a sense reversing the order of concern:

> The Greek word 'therapeutes' means attendant, servant. The earliest therapeutic measure was devoted to driving out the demons from the bodies of the victims. The method usually consisted in the reciting of charms or magic over the ailing parts or over the sick person...by a priestly man, a primitive counterpart of the principal therapeutic actor, the auxiliary ego, in a theatre for the psychodrama. The drama, long before it was a place for the presentation of art and entertainment, was a place for therapeutics, the sick coming to it for catharsis. Aristotle defines catharsis in his *Poetics* as follows: "The task of the tragedy is to produce through the exercise of fear and pity liberation from such

> emotions." Aristotle expected the catharsis to take place in the spectator. The modern point of view...is that the tragedy, to be truly cathartic material has to be created by the actor-patients themselves out of their own psychic stuff, and not by a playwright. *(Psychodrama,* pp. 179-80)

So Moreno wanted to get back to the generous realm of therapeutic potential that the drama had within its initial core. And in archetypal terms, we could add that the stories people portray in instant dramatic form often partake of ancient material. The very imperfection of the psychodramatic production is from Moreno's perspective a virtue. He does not think 'finished' work is all that valuable from the therapeutic perspective. It's a remarkable position and of course takes scant consideration of the many other factors that enter into the drama's history as an art form. Moreno is concerned with the drama's relationship with life and how the reinvigorated spontaneous psyche can come to know itself and heal itself within these new forms of interpersonal action. The actual life of the person involved in the work becomes the focus of that activity, not the aesthetic values associated with a finished art work.

*

These lines of inquiry have been the subject of numerous debates for some years now, and in the 60s spawned many experimental theatre operations, the most famous being The Living Theater. I think it could be argued that much of the intense improvisational theatre as well as so-called "happenings" were instigated by an interest in psychodrama. Another name for Moreno's 'cultural conserve' was the much maligned 'establishment.' There is a passionate exchange between Andre Gregory (one of the celebrated directors of the 1960s) and Wallace Shawn in Louis Malle's (1981) film *My Dinner with Andre* in which Andre regards people as currently so asleep that only the most intense experience will affect them. He goes on to say that the theatre is no longer a living thing and people will need to go through explosive and toxic things like being buried alive in order to feel anything at all: "What I think I experienced [after a ritual burial with Grotowski's group in Poland] was for the first time in my life to know what it means to be truly alive. And that's very frightening because with that comes an immediate awareness of death. They go hand in hand...."

My own sense, having worked in the theatre at many levels—including some of the resident professional theatres—is that traditional theatre *does* present serious problems for performers who must go through the strenuous work of learning a script or finding a way to 'make it new' over the run of a show. Often, from my psychologically-based position, my truly creative work took place backstage where the great variety of my interests had a chance to be played out. And the relationships among fellow actors as they are getting into costume, makeup and role are often undergoing a deeper more vital submergence in life while onstage relationships can remain somewhat static.

Though this has many variables, if the show is actually a 'living' entity, the roles onstage can have a dynamic and a vigor that is infinitely renewable.

I remember a strong backstage relationship developing between two actors (at La Jolla Playhouse) who had very different attitudes about the Pope's role in a current (1986) situation in Nicaragua. The Hispanic actor felt the Pope had abandoned his leadership position by refusing to acknowledge the Sandinista Government. The Polish actor, by contrast, was very weary of the Communist rule in his country and did not see the Pope's attitude as contradictory at all. Besides, he knew the Pope personally, and was fond of talking about John Paul's activities in the Polish theatre as both actor and playwright. Some of the exchanges between the two actors (while dressed in 18th Century costume) were very heated and in many ways more interesting and expressive than their onstage relationships. And as a spectator and colleague, I felt I was seeing them clearly in their totalities: the spontaneous nuance that came from their private personalities was probably more meaningful to me personally, though I admired their acting abilities as well.

*

And so we have heard from these voices. What is the relationship between art and therapy, between conscious and unconscious, between making a living and making a life? We want meaning and we want a way to work in the world. Could we say that Moreno and Stanislavsky wrote from the perspective of their professions, the one a medical psychologist and the other a theatre director? And aren't both activities concerned with the truth of man's nature, each in its own way finding a language of inquiry and a participatory activity that is the cornerstone of the work? Moreno found in the therapeutic theatre something essential to man's processes: spontaneity and creativity go to the heart of a person's needs. And Stanislavsky discovered in theatre art a rallying of creative individuals who "want to move forward because their inner powers grow strong and develop, and search for new ways to express themselves in creative action." (1961, p. 91) We could talk here about two different individuals, two different psychological types, with two different pictures of the world. As Jung has remarked:

> If we do not fashion for ourselves a picture of the world, we do not see ourselves either, who are the faithful reflections of that world. Only when mirrored in our picture of the world can we see ourselves in the round.... Yet we know the immensities of space better than we know our own depths, where—even though we do not understand it—we can listen directly to the throb of creation itself. (Ibid., p. 380)

And Emerson in *Self Reliance*: "Insist on yourself; never imitate. Your own gift you can present every moment with the cumulative force of a whole life's cultivation...." (Emerson, 1909, p. 84)

*

## STANISLAVSKY, MORENO, AND A MEDIATING EGO: A TRIALOGUE

Stanislavsky. I need to make art.

Moreno. It's therapy we're after.

Ego. You both seek culture, a sense of the eternal, one with text and endless rehearsal, the other with all the eruptions of spontaneity.

Stan. I'm not concerned with therapy.

Mor. I'm tired of the hubbub about the cultural conserve.

Ego. Abandon the squabbling. Become one again. Find the comic infernally in your differences. Confess your vital interest in the human being and have done with it.

Mor. I'm convinced that Everyman is more profound.

Stan. You are a boob.

Mor. You are an elitist and a critic.

Ego. You are both merely energies in our drama.

## 8
## THE ACTOR AND THE SOUL

Coming as I did from the professional theatre, it was natural that I would want to find a professional community that sparked a similar creative process. The theatre is a great home for souls; we test the distances in theatre, we make way in text and gesture; we dig down and find meaning in bodies, voices, the way a plot turns. It is an exciting world, one in which people play parts and the whole is enjoined to celebrate an author's vision. In our workshops the attempt is to find a form that is made up by the actors who have come to celebrate a spontaneous theatre existence, and the subjects come from within the personal and archetypal histories of the participants.

The variety of subject matter and form in archetypal drama is tremendous. We find in each drama the seeds of possible journeys that can change lives. Persons often introduce a Hermes figure, or a soul guide that can take them on a tour of some underworld they are entering. This is often a natural extension of the psychic material being explored. The guide may be the personification of an inner dimension like Virgil to Dante in the Divine Comedy or she may be some kind of subtle form of companion, embodying an intuition or a possible direction. She may contain trickster elements and may express an ambivalence that does not give off an Apollonian clarity. But she will hopefully shed new light—even sometimes dark light—on the person's journey, allowing an internal dialogue to be available every step of the way. In the archetypal drama workshops, we often give persons this guide instead of the more traditional 'double' of classical psychodrama. The guide offers an inner reflectiveness and a camaraderie that is often very helpful, especially in transitional moments in the unfolding drama.

In our workshops, we usually attempt to personify the inner guides (and all other figures), extending the imaginal activity into as many potentialities as we can muster. And this means that inanimate objects can be personified as well. In a recent drama, our protagonist was uncovering the particulars of a dream and she came to an old family heirloom, a chest of drawers: in each drawer was another level of her mother's family history. She was able to open drawers and re-examine objects that had been inherited from her mother. It was a strange and powerful passage in her work, as she (with eyes closed) opened the successive drawers, detailing what each contained, and speaking for the contents, bringing the chest to life, giving it vocal intensity and meaning.

*

There is a recurring theme in theatre work, and in therapy as well, dealing with the question as to whether one is essentially alone or connected to others in one's soul. There may be a connection with how we see ourselves, our self image. How do you see yourself? Were you treated badly as a child? Is it a humiliating image? Is it now too late to find another image? A man may be in conflict with different parts of himself. He may have an internal critic that wants its way with him. There might be a child.

Critic. You make me ill. You are worthless. You can't do anything right. You have sinned and nothing will redeem you.

Child. Nobody pays attention to me.

Ego. What is all this noise?

Critic. You're ineffective, you're ugly, you can't put anything together.

Child. I want to have fun, I want to do something in the sun.

Ego. I want an admirable image of myself. I want to stand tall. It's all right to find in the extraordinary—the past, the classical ages, the pure exemplar of rarefied mankind—something to take hold of and cherish.

*

In our workshops, we let the soul gravitate to whatever myth or metaphorical agency is spontaneously constellated. We let the myth lead, giving us a direction as we pursue an inner course. As analytic tradition has shown again and again, the psyche will produce its own materials, sometimes through dreams, sometimes through spontaneous association, sometimes through slips of the tongue. Recently, a member of our group mentioned fear in the context of blockage, and we immediately gave his fear a personified form and he discovered that this 'inner fear' has a determinable existence and specific personality that indeed halts many of his approaches to a life beyond his current one.

In the archetypal workshops we find our way to useful fictions, or 'guiding fictions,' as Adler called them. The idea is not to literalize goals, but to keep them moving fictionally, guided by the psyche's intrinsic imaginal tendencies. As Hillman (1983) says in *Healing Fiction*:

> Inasmuch as a goal is a guiding fiction showing a way, it is a healing fiction. To be healed is that goal which takes one into therapy, and we are healed of that goal when we recognize it as a fiction.... This deliteralized method of healing, so ironic, slippery, paradoxical, that seems to fulfill and defeat our striving at the same time, bespeaks the mercurial consciousness of Hermes, Guide of Souls, Guide of Ways. (p. 105)

And so the way, the journey, the guided tour of the fictional underground or dramatic stage becomes the goal, which is imbued with paradox from the beginning. It is a way of finding a fictional or imaginal home and it requires a way of working that keeps the way open, does not literalize the goal either as personal maturity or actualization, but keeps the imagination alert to its next line, its next gesture, or its next error.

A major component of Adler's theory is Communal Feeling, *Gemeinschaftsgefuhl,* or social interest. Our work attempts to affirm the soul's deep need for community and allows a multiplicity of contributions from the entire ensemble.

Moreno called his original psychodrama theatre 'the theatre of truth,' which finds a similar resonance in Herman Hesse's 'Magic Theatre' in *The Steppenwolf*. And what is the meaning of our group? It is the ground plan for a large geographical and inward journey that takes in a whole host of historical and cultural contexts, unlimited in scope and origin. The world become one's backyard, one's shining hopes riding the horse of a different color—trapped in Anna Karenina's dilemma between her child and her lover, split between the imagined perfect beauty of Romeo & Juliet's romance and the facts of their star-crossed affair, caught in the unbending humor of Don Quixote fighting windmills against all odds. We want to live in a fullness of the soul's quest, its endless permutations and capacity for love and ferment. Each occasion is a new adventure of work, a way to find in our mutual concerns the material for a fresh look at our worlds.

*

The issue of time is important in our dramatic work, for in the drama—and in this I include psychodrama and traditional forms of drama as well as our archetypal drama—there is the recurring sense that another order of time occurs. In *The Sacred and The Profane*, Eliade (1959) says: "Hence religious man lives in two kinds of time, of which the more important, sacred time, appears under the paradoxical aspect of circular time, reversible and recoverable, a sort of eternal mythical present that is periodically reintegrated by means of rites." (p. 70)

The drama allows time to be reborn in the same way that religious rituals are known to do this. Time is born again at each performance of a show, at each enactment in the archetypal psychodrama. The creative act coincides with the imagination of something happening in cosmic space, in which "time gushes forth with the first appearance of a new category of existents." (Eliade, 1959, p. 76) In a sense mythic potential becomes an event that is now present and reactualized in some kind of primordial time. The attempt to make this happen in film has made some of its greatest moments, as seen in some of Fellini's work, especially in *8½*, and more recently in Terry Gilliam's (1991) *The Fisher King*. Eliade, again: "By symbolically participating in the annihilation and re-creation of the world, man was created anew; he was reborn, for he began a new life." (1959, p. 79)

And so what I call 'the festive wellsprings' of archetypal drama give us back this sense of time in which we are participating in a kind of eternally opening presence, in which our hearts are prefigured in a mythic unfolding that holds for us the secret of joyous communication. We enact a pure event, the kind Rilke searched for, the kind Corbin talks of in his rapturous commentary on Ibn Arabi's prayers and angelology. We want to uncover this sense of the sacred in the concrete human event, in the heart's attachment to soul's depths.

*

*The work started with Joan's eating disorder. We split her concerns into the Angry Woman and the Submissive Woman. We put a desk between them. Angry Woman told Submissive Woman (who was also the dieter concerned about her appearance) that being fat was important because it kept the men away. She cast a double. Asked what this scenario was actually dealing with, she said memory and we cast Memory and the protagonist presented Memory. Memory said that Joan was a pretty child and that she did not deserve to have her past unlocked. Joan reversed roles with Memory several times. Finally, Joan said she saw the image of the piece of the puzzle she was looking for. Her male relatives had flipped a coin when she was five years old to see which of them would incest her first. She then cast her self as a young child and told her that she was not responsible for what they did to her. She embraced her young self and there was much weeping and consolation.*

Joan had undergone a deep sense of transformation. She wanted to go further in her work than she had ever previously gone. In the first two days of this workshop, she sat in a kind of tense, remote state, not much vigor or ease in her demeanor. Now she was alerted to inner processes that stirred her toward new dimensions of feeling and understanding. (The process of dramatizing her condition spurred this.) The breakthrough brought with it a new aspect of knowledge that was necessary for her survival. And the group became for her a subtle inner support system that gave her the strength to push ahead in her work. The resistance to the actual memory with all its overlay of fantastic and archetypal components was so powerful that she needed the agency of the collective—in this case the gathered ensemble of dramatic helpers—to get to the ground of her work. She found the terrible image which was simultaneously a deep darkness and an opportunity to revision her own psychic condition.

These moments of shared breakthrough are the essence of this work. It finds the self deeply connected with its own origins and in the presence of community where there is a vibrancy, a sense of the holy and a feeling of being at home in the world that is beyond words. D.H. Lawrence (1921) wrote of this sense in *Fantasia of the Unconscious*:

> To be alone with one's own soul.... This, and the joy of it, is the real goal of love. My own soul, and myself. Not my ego, my conceit of myself. But my very soul.... Not to be questing any more. Not to be yearning, seeking, hoping, desiring, aspiring. But to pause, and be alone. (p. 168)

This profound sense of aloneness that allows the community as a whole to support solitude is something unique and paradoxical in this kind of group engagement. As in 'the private moment' in the Stanislavsky method, there is a sense of deep personal aloneness in the midst of the vibrant warmth of the ensemble. There is an awakening of the deepest self and a satisfaction in its creative turns. It is a return to the soul's ritual center, a place that is deeply quiescent and satisfying. The protagonist has regathered a living presence, a place to rest after the focused quest.

## ꙮ 9 ꙮ
## ARCHETYPAL ORIGINS OF TRAGEDY

*Saying yes to life even in its strangest and hardest problems.... (The Birth of Tragedy,* Nietzsche)

*The ordinary technique of the dream is that it gets the patient into the archetypal situation in order to cure him, the situation of the suffering godman or the situation of human tragedy. This was the effect of Greek tragedy.* (Jung, CW 8)

The tragic takes us close to the original power of dramatic art. In it the full complexity of human experience comes up against those spiritual and social forces that confront every human being. Most of us search for lives where we have the sense of truly belonging—to others, to our work and to the world. But in the tragedy, we find that the world nears a terrible uncertainty from which all must teeter. Nothing is safe, neither knowledge nor relationship. Hamlet, Oedipus, Lear, Medea—all are torn from their advancement and must rely on a psychical thread, from which they all hang. They are all under great pressure to act and to understand action, yet all fall from their earlier status into a quagmire of impossible circumstances. Each character reaches a state in which a new beginning is imperative, a state in which life and death enter a dramatic action that propels the tragedy toward towering poetry and a majesty that transcends human circumstance.

In tragedy, the play plunges us into a chaos of powerful forces in which there is a great struggle that leads to new foundations for truth. Nietzsche says in *The Birth of Tragedy*:

> The metaphysical solace [that] life is at bottom indestructibly joyful and powerful, was expressed most concretely in the chorus of satyrs, nature beings who dwell behind all civilization and preserve their identity through every change of generations and historical movements. ( p. 50)

*

Archetypal Drama's relationship with the origins of tragedy is important to grasp. There is in both realms the desire for rich emotional and experiential depth, as well as a wild and radical vitality at the heart of the creative process itself. We know that Greek theatre arose in connection with the cult of Dionysus, who was supposed to enter the theatre and take possession of his worshipers through a form of mystical communion. We now think of various kinds of enthusiasms and inspirations including wine-bibing and sexual potency (and its modern overindulgences in action adventure films) as part of the Dionysian framework. The majesty of the towering tragedies still speaks to us today, and the mad god who inspired the original essence of the masked actor still affects us. The tremendous enrichment that the drama has given us is reason alone to acknowledge Dionysus and his inexhaustible and life-affirming depth.

In her *Archetypal Patterns of Poetry* (1934), Maud Bodkin talks about the 'tragic exultation' that we feel at the end of *Hamlet*:

> If the spiritual power...be conceived psychologically as the awakened sense of our common nature in its active emotional phase, then our exultation in the death of Hamlet is related in direct line of descent to the religious exultation felt by the primitive group that made sacrifice of the divine king or sacred animal, the representative of the tribal life, and, by the communion of its shed blood, felt that life strengthened and renewed. Hamlet, though he dies, is immortal, because he is the representative and creature of the immortal life of the race. (p. 21)

There is thus a union with a larger whole, a transpersonal experience which is the essence of the archetypal ground of collective experience. We have in the tragic hero a multi-layered ambivalence in which he is aggressively assertive of his individual soul and at the same time there is the sense ultimately of a submission to a larger destiny that takes the hero back into the collective mystery.

In tragedy, there is the recurring theme of limits that may not be transgressed. And there is ambiguity. In melodrama, there is clear villainy. In tragedy, all can be justified and no one need be just. Antigone is right, but Creon is as well. Tragedy is tension, conflict, and a great deal of paradox. Tragedy occurs when a protagonist enters into conflict with a divine order, personified by a god or incarnated in a social frame. Oedipus transgressed the limits of the divine order; Hamlet cannot bring himself to face the further defeats awaiting him should he complete the Ghost's demands. The revolt is justified, but then the order is necessary for the maintenance of the social or religious world view.

But what now in our age that seems bogged down in its own inconsolable dimensions is the possible need for tragic experience? Stanley Cavell (1987) in his essay on *King Lear* argues: "A purpose of tragedy remains unchanged: to make us practical, capable of acting. It used to do that by showing the natural limitations of action. Now its work is not to purge us of fear and terror, but to make us capable of feeling them again." (p. 118)

In the archetypal drama workshop, through improvisations directed toward our deepest concerns, we reach new levels of powerful emotion. We invent it, and we go where the energy and the feeling take us, and this has curious twists and turns. We might be connected with the vague splits of Hermes or the darkness of Hades. Often, in the workshop, there's a theme struck that moves past the personal to some universal meaning.

*Andrea had observed a dog being abandoned on the freeway. She had come to the workshop very upset. We created a drama in which she addressed the deep cruelty of mankind, in the form of shadow creatures. She was able to reverse roles and get into the most sordid attitudes about life. The risk was that she would go so far down into the Hades of her drama that it would sink her utterly. We had a photograph projector that we decided to use to represent a kind of light in darkness. We turned the room lights off and Andrea addressed the light, as a projective archetypal source of beauty and power. She was able to close the sequence with some light work, so to speak. She felt that there was still redeeming potential in the species. But we all had the sense that she was dealing with ultimate questions, a battle between (in Jungian terms) collective shadow and the forces of the self. It was dramatically a fair fight and she had gone the distance with it.*

This gathering of extremes was a difficult occasion for all of us. An actual event was presented and the shame and mean-spiritedness of the act (of leaving the dog to die) was really disturbing for everyone. Andrea could not enter the group's work because of her emotional state and so our work centered on dealing with her situation. She was experiencing the confusion and rage of a tragic situation, represented by the dog's plight. And so, spontaneously, we got hold of this emotionally-charged problem and constructed a dramatic form that attempted to deal with this storm of powerful feeling that had entered her processes.

*

A word should be said about the special quality of affection that seems to grow up around both theatre groups and the archetypal drama workshops. The people who come together in a creative spirit find, I think, a parallel to the Christian concept of *agape,* in its deep sense of spiritual communion. Erik Erikson (1964) in a paranthetical passage in *Young Man Luther* talks about this in another context:

> I saw a small and transient example of the gaiety of *agape* only two decades ago, in a small pueblo in our Southwest. Though excommunicated from the the Roman Church for an act of collective disobedience, the pueblo was preparing for a religious holiday, I think Easter. The men were mending the adobe walls of the church, the young people formed a chain to hand buckets of water from the brook, and the women, dressed in gay colors, were scrubbing and washing the church. Where the altar had been, an elder sat, wrinkled, shrewd, dignified; he was the oldest and newest priest, and was supervising the construction of a madonna, an enormous ball of colorful cloth topped by a tiny crowned head. Somewhere on her global bosom there lay a tiny pink baby doll. Instead of candles this goddess was surrounded by magnificent cornstalks. One could not help feeling that the concordant gaiety

> which bound these people together in the improvisation of a religion, combining the best of the old and the new, was a response to having been freed from the supervision of the law. In ignoring the excommunication they gained a gay energy from the historical vacuum. (pp. 179-80)

The work can become thus a holiday of transcendence, a holy freedom from the law. The reformulation of what the work is is sometimes the liberating ingredient. The work defined as promiseful play, of an occasion to free the soul for a deep searching ride in inner space, makes the potential for 'gaiety' or fun an accompaniment to the therapeutic enterprise. The drama is a great condensation and celebration of meaningful play.

The theatre—and tragedy in particular—has had to deal with the tremendous advances of scientific knowledge in the twentieth century. The theatre has had to cope with various forms of collapsing values and crises of faith. A major anti-modernist who attempted to create tragedy was Eugene O'Neill. In a telling comment on the idea of spiritual awakening in America, O'Neill wrote:

> A soul is being born...and when a soul enters, tragedy enters with it. Suppose some day we should suddenly see with the clear eye of a soul the true valuation of all our triumphant brass band materialism.... What a colossal, ironic 100 per cent American tragedy that would be—what? Tragedy not native to our soil? Why, we are tragedy—the most appalling yet written and unwritten. (Gelb and Gelb, pp. 486-7)

O'Neill and others have attempted to re-discover this ancient profound dramatic expression. A drama of spiritual conflict, often echoing the dark emotionally savage dramas of August Strindberg, becomes the realm of this kind of work. And a recurring event in tragedy, as well as in our workshops, is the enactment of a recognition that changes the protagonist in some powerful way. It often results in the altering of the course of action and a propulsion toward spiritual awakening or a new form of soulfulness.

*In the workshop at the ASGPP (American Society of Group Psychotherapy and Psychodrama) Conference in New York, two men chose Vincent Van Gogh for their enactments of historical characters. One chose Vincent as a young man, and the predominant element in his character was fire. The other chose the older Vincent, the Van Gogh bound to his own wheel of fate, struggling against time and madness. The two protagonists faced each other and each interviewed the other, and it was as if two extraordinary entities were embodying large dimensions of the modern soul. The young Vincent stormed across the stage, talking of the blazing sense he had of imagined visions that he would transform into paintings. The older Vincent, still in a state of creative ferment though less vigorous than his younger component, talked of his failure to find a sustaining position in the world, and how his psychosis was affecting his ability to stay in the human realm. There was an essential religious feel to both positions and we asked questions of the two historical embodiments, and they answered in character, each detailing an heroic quest that met with some success and some failure, but the emotional quality of the effort was consistently ennobled and tragic.*

There is a recurring sense that the soul is at home in the depths of its own tragedy and sorrow, that it cares as deeply for depth and suffering as anything else. Perhaps there are states of hysterical grief that touch the soul in such a potent way that they are a form of celebration and relief. In the workshops this often comes home:

*Linda's daughter Kim's anorexia had become nothing but tragic to her. There seemed to be no therapy. Kim despised herself and was thoroughly convinced that her mother was just as bad off as herself. Kim scolded her mother vehemently and was not convinced that she would regather self-respect or health. As mother reversed roles with daughter, it was obvious that there was no love lost between them. She bore a terrible grudge but vowed to try to develop a richer form of communication. No telling if the tragedy would reverse itself, only a hope from the protagonist that her daughter come to a brighter sense of her own possibilities. Some form of gentle hope moved Linda toward the impossible affection that strained her relationship with Kim. There was a powerful opposition in Kim's very being. She saw her mother as hypocritical and there was the sense of bitter entrenchment. Mother was the indicted 'cause' of Kim's excesses with dieting. And the final scene between the two involved Linda saying good-bye to Kim and Kim going out into the world to find her own progress.*

Linda, our protagonist, becomes a poet of the intrapsychic theatre in whose power the experience of the drama comes to life. Nietzsche says: "All one needs in order to be a poet is the ability to have a lively action going on before one continually, to live surrounded by hosts of spirits. To be a dramatist all one needs is the urge to transform oneself and speak out of strange bodies and souls." (Ibid., p. 55)

And thus a sort of projection occurs: out of oneself there come various dramatic manifestations of one's own innerness. Another entity steps into existence from deep within the dramatist or perhaps from some depersonalized aspect of the universal archetypal. And in our archetypal drama workshops, these 'strange bodies and souls' take the form of personified energies that are played by auxiliaries in the group or chorus of players. And the play of elements leads us to a dialectical solution to the play's original propositions. Nietzsche speaks of what he calls a 'triumphant serenity' which prevails in the towering tragedies. Thus the great horror of the conflicts of Oedipus or King Lear brings us ultimately into a realm of consolation in which prevails a sense of peace and order after great suffering.

*Len's drama was about the relationship with the Great Mother. He wanted to create a piece that allowed an interplay between his personal world and the archetypal world.*

*We first cast The Damaged Child, aged 18 months. Len presented this child as having had a very disturbed dissatisfying beginning. He then cast his Biological Mother and she talked about her marriage and the problems she had with her husband and children.*

*He then cast and presented The Great Mother, with whom he had a strong relationship, but he needed to know more from her about how her energy could help him with his ongoing life. He then cast his current girlfriend, Gina, and she talked about how she often felt smothered by Len and how she wanted to continue their relationship, perhaps even have a child together, but she exhorted Len to give her room when she needed to be by herself. Len talked to her in a quiet voice, trying to reassure her that he indeed understood what she needed from him. Len proceeded with his dialogue with the Great Mother, and she reminded him that he had to learn something about sacrifice if he was to succeed with his relationships.*

*Len cast Sacrifice and this character was sardonic and powerful, said she would dominate him, turn everything he did into sacrifice if he let her. Ken said he understood what Sacrifice was implying, but that he did not feel he needed to let her control his destiny. His Biological Mother said that Sacrifice had been with her always and she had let Sacrifice determine her life. She had sacrificed her life for her husband and her family and she told Gina, his current girlfriend, that she should be wary of overdetermining her life with sacrifice.*

*Len, his Companion and the Director stood in the center of the stage and talked about what ingredient might bring all these forces together. Len suggested Love, possibly, but then went on to say that Intimacy was the major player here. Len cast Intimacy and she took the stage with terrific energy, coming close to every other character and ultimately putting them together in a kind of huddle that rose to an occasion of brilliance that startled us all. Like a vast heated ball of affection, Intimacy warmed the historical and present figures, shaping a soft landing for us all, giving Len a vision that felt transcendent, serene and complete.*

## ꟳ 10 ꟳ
## RESEARCH OF THE HEART

*And it is this sharing, this mutual guarantee, which is the work of theophanic prayer, itself 'creative' in the same way as the theophanic Imagination because in every instance it brings about a recurrence of Creation.* (Henry Corbin)

To find in the imaginative mix of our creative work a theophany or vision of the divine is to move our discussion to the field of creative religious studies where Corbin's work stands as exemplar of the conjunction possible between psychological and religious discourse. Corbin (1969) writes of 'the heart' as the organ "which produces true knowledge, comprehensive intuition, the gnosis of God and divine mysteries...." This 'subtile organ' is the means of perceiving new theophanies or revelations of the Divine Being. Similarly, in our active dramatic imaginings we are seeking to put the heart to work to achieve a true knowledge of things, a knowledge denied to the intellect alone. The work requires a psycho-spiritual capacity to render experience in metaphorical and transcendent terms. The testimony of mystics like Ibn Arabi (the 12th century Sufi poet) helps fecundate our own work, giving us transferrable means to understand how our own capacity to imagine dialogically stems from an ancient use of the imagination:

> The spiritual progression from simple belief to the mystic state is accomplished through an increasing capacity for making oneself present to the vision by the Imagination: progressing from mental vision by typification by way of dream vision, to verification in the station of imaginative witnessing vision.... (Ibid., p. 232)

Corbin (Ibid.) speaks of "the universal and liberating function of the active imagination: to typify, to transmute everything into an Image-symbol by perceiving the correspondence between the hidden and the visible...." (p. 243) The symbolic structure can establish magnitudes of existence on planes entirely other than our ordinary conscious experience. We can speak of artistic or dramatic truth as having a certain recurrent theme of imaginative presence that informs the creative existence of our characters or images.

And language partakes of the imaginal perhaps best exemplified in the work of Shakespeare. In *The Tempest*, Caliban, denizen of the magic island, talks of the enchanted music of the isle:

> Be not afeard, the isle is full of noises,
> Sounds, and sweet airs, that give delight and hurt not.
> Sometimes a thousand twangling instruments
> Will hum about mine ears; and sometimes voices,

That if I then had wak'd after long sleep,
Will make me sleep again, and then in dreaming,
The clouds methought would open, and show riches
Ready to drop upon me, that when I wak'd
I cried to dream again. (III. ii. 135-43)

Just as the soul is at home in the dream world, so the essence of the human quest for meaning is aligned with creative imagination. Archetypal art therapist Shaun McNiff (1989) has written: "The external motivation activates the inner. If we want to encourage people to make art, then the best thing to do is expose them to a dynamic studio, and help them to feel comfortable and confident in it." ( p. 126) In the archetypal drama workshops, we start from the position that the world is remarkably open to experiment and that whatever presents itself as inner experience or questions and hunches about the world can be translated into dramatic events. The work seems ever to involve both an inner and an outer dimension, so that even when we are working with archetypal figures or abstract ideas, there is still something deeply personal being processed.

*Tom had recently won a great deal of money in Las Vegas. His work centered on finding out what kind of energy was responsive to him when he was winning. We cast a central energy form which he called Unknown Energy. He reversed roles with it. It said it was part of him but that he could not control it. We then added a Feminine Dimension to it, and a dual system emerged and the two parts dialogued. Tom mentioned how fear gets in the way of his relation to Unknown Energy. We cast Fear and she told him that Fear's job was to get in the way of his other relationships. He then mentioned Gladness and Understanding as essentials in his relationship with Unknown Energy and we cast them. They were supportive, but said they could not be active when he was fearful. He closed with a dialogue with Unknown Energy, asking if he could work together with it. Unknown Energy was supportive and said the relationship could grow. Tom said he was willing to try to keep the relationship alive.*

*

*The perception of therapy as an art practiced by artists helps to integrate the identity of the art therapist.... The closeting, or separation of the therapist's identity as an artist will no longer be necessary. The stereotype of the artist who is afraid or reluctant to inquire into the psychological process of creation for fear of knowing too much and losing, or altering the conflictual chemistry that motivates expression, may be a thing of the past. (McNiff, 1989, pp 122-23)*

The call to deepen one's own involvement in the art making process is here an important step in the expressive therapy story. The usual thinking in this light is that the therapeutic worker has somehow lost his connection to art and has gone out to pasture to do therapy. On the contrary, if the artist-healer can find an integration between his dual identities, then there can be an enrichment of the discovery process for everyone in the group. The discovery permitted in the conjunction between art and therapy is a development which has added great riches to our expressive work. Sometimes, as I recently discovered at the wonderful Center for Expressive Arts & Psychotherapy in Tucson, the constellated experience is one of entering the domain of the theatre, with its capacity to move the body and soul to new extensions of joy and meaning. And in this context the space itself is important: persons entering the Tucson Center experience a lovely polished oak dance floor and walls filled with oil paintings by local artists. A person becomes located in a world of expressive freedom; the actor archetype is engaged and beckoned and work emerges with a naturalness that is sometimes sublime. Given the right atmosphere, characters of the sacred come into play with a splendid ease.

*

In dealing with the relationship between alchemy and psychology, Jung regularly reminds us of "the polaristic structure of the psyche, which it shares with all natural processes. Natural processes are phenomena of energy, constantly arising out of a 'less probable state of polar tension.'" (CW 12, p. xvi)

Likewise, the archetypal drama events attempt to duplicate or parallel this kind of polarity. We initiate our work with a dialogue between two conditions, two opposites, two dynamic elements in the psychic life of our protagonists. And the synthesis is always grounded in paradox—of known and unknown, of real and artificial, of base and stupendous. It is the realm of Hermes, forever afoot in the arcane symbolical wedding dance of the alchemical opposites.

*

At another level Smith and Berg (1987), in *Paradoxes of Group Life*, deal extensively with various ramifications of paradox as a function of group dynamics:

> When discussing the paradox of identity, we noted how easy it is for individuals to adopt a heroic stance toward the group. Out of the belief that the only way to become one's own person is by gaining mastery of the group comes the struggle between self and group, David and Goliath. In the paradox of individuality, we find a complementary dynamic in the heroic, expressed in archetypal form. On the one side, we find expressions of the collective good, the call for commitment to a common goal.... On the other side, we find the virtues of individuality, creativity, freedom of expression.... (pp 101-2)

In our archetypal drama groups there is a tension between the group and the individual; and yet the potential to overcome the ambivalence is strong because we can put the entire collective to work on a shared journey that (metaphorically) involves not just this particular temporal group but all humankind, symbolized by the group's pulling together to stage the elements of an individual's story. The heroic effort (in the tradition of a Ulysses on a quest) then becomes part of the fabric of the form we have put to work, and the formal elements are capable of blending with the individual's will to imagine (and stage) an intuitive entity which will deal in depth with her inner quest.

*Sara had been a dancer but after her auto accident she was unable to dance. She had suffered some spinal damage that also affected her bladder so that she had to deal with various kinds of physical distress. Her drama consisted of setting up a dialogue with the part of her in pain and the part of her that wanted to console herself. The part of her that was in pain talked about a shattered life, physical disability and an almost despairing attitude. The consoling part moved very close to the suffering part and told her that she was capable of getting beyond this troubled state. She reversed roles several times and there arose the sense that there was a closeness and care between these oppositional elements that gave the rest of us the perception that they were working together and that there would be some hopeful future for her in the midst of the troubling obstacles. She was learning to dance in a new way.*

These figures become transparent when activated by the imagination through dialogue. The heart's work becomes the entry into the phenomenal world of imaginal forms that come alive through dialogue. There is a metamorphosis here, a movement of creative manifestation that comes through the vocal and visual enactment between the two positions, in this case a painful dimension and a consoling dimension. Each position is a necessary precondition to this particular drama, permitting a compassionate flow of emotion, allowing a renewing concrete instant to enter a full presence, a moment when all the senses are engaged in the surprising acceptance mixed with seriousness that this internal witnessing gathered and expressed.

## ꕥ 11 ꕥ
## THE PERFORMANCE CONNECTION

*The actor who undertakes an act of self-penetration, who reveals himself and sacrifices the innermost part of himself—the most painful, that which is not intended for the eyes of the world—must be able to manifest the least impulse. He must be able to express, through sound and movement, those impulses which waver on the borderline between dream and reality.* (Jerzy Grotowski)

The desire to perform, it seems to me, must have roots in the desire for self-mastery and artistic composure. The work of the actor becomes a way to illuminate in speech and gesture the inner life of a person in communication with others, and ultimately, with an audience. The actor's work also becomes a ceremony in which others assist: other actors, designers, director—all putting themselves into the force field in which the actor attempts to dig into the human condition in a way that illuminates it. Brook (1968) goes on and talks of the major model for his own conception of theatre at its best:

> The model, as always is Shakespeare. His aim continually is holy, metaphysical, yet he never makes the mistake of staying too long on the highest plane. He knew how hard it is for us to keep company with the absolute.... (p. 56)

What we are looking for in practice in archetypal drama is a form to reconceive our own life stories in terms of dramatic imagination. We want to replay life poetically, giving each individual actor the chance to "clap (his) hands and sing," to quote Yeats. We believe in the essential creative energy that the drama allows us to stage. We find a metaphorical engagement with figures that produce both conflict and catharsis.

So the task becomes the same one an artist is forced to face with each blank page, empty space or empty canvas. What does this particular time and space give me in terms of my work? What are its essences? Its forces that will conjure an image or a phrase? What rapturous inclination will give me the momentum to put my signature on this piece of material? Am I up to it? Can I do it? Find in my own psyche a semblance of power and reflection that will bring out of the chaos of my desire and suffering a substantial yield, driving me further into life, giving me something to stand on. It is the ever present challenge, the quiet before the storm. The expression, the 'squeezing out' of form comes from within, from as Jung says "something which I do not control." And these independent entities, or archetypal figures that are generated by dreams or fantasy are given real respect—a place to dwell in the creative kingdom, a place to inhabit and be heard. And the body comes to the momentum of the creative intelligence and there is a blossoming of concern, the world come alive with sensation, feeling, intellect, and intuitive powers. The psyche can find a home in the therapeutic theatre, and it can feel as though there is a continuity with time, and a resurgence of timing that brings us back to the timelessness of archetypal dramatic form.

## A DIGRESSION ON THE AMERICAN THEATRE

Much of modern drama works to comprehend the vitality and decay of an inner world. Willy Loman (in *Death of a Salesman*) lives in a dream world and is seemingly trapped in it. He believes in athletic gods like his son Biff when he was young and he glories in the phony advertised folly of a 'simonized' American Dream, but it's destroying him, giving him a form of inner suffering that is both profound and pathetic. Willy, like so many of O'Neill's and Tennessee Williams's heroes, is losing on two fronts, the inner and the outer. Relationship is not working. Willy is losing ground with his sons and his work world. Willy's world is not unlike the dream world that Hickey in O'Neill's *The Iceman Cometh* continues to condemn. Unreality and pipe-dreams rule the world of Harry Hope's bums, but the alternative that both Hickey and Larry Slade prescribe may in fact be just as awful a course to follow. What do they offer? Slade provokes young Parritt to suicide and Hickey's reforming message is simply intolerable to Harry's dreamers. There is no good will in Hickey and he is offering an impossible solution: death as an answer to unreality. Hickey has killed his wife because she was the depository of his guilt and self-loathing. Now he's free to haunt the drunks. As Josie in *The Moon for the Misbegotten* says to the passed out Jim Tyrone: "That's right. Sleep in peace, my darling. (Then with sudden anguished longing) Oh, Jim, Jim, maybe my love could still save you, if you could want it enough! (She shakes her head) No, that can never be.... God forgive me, it's a fine end to all my scheming, to sit here with the dead hugged to my breast, and the silly mug of the moon grinning down, enjoying the joke!"

Which brings us to this great archetypal moment in American drama: Jim Tyrone becomes the child at the mother's breast, the Pieta-like union of that ancient pair. O'Neill is perhaps asserting this as the genuine model of authentic human love. Physically and emotionally Josie is supporting this dying man, nourishing him and forgiving him as he teeters at the edge of oblivion. Josie knows how damaged Jim is, deprived of love for so long and condemning himself for past sins. But her holding him offers him a kind of symbolic rebirth, though she knows he is in fact near death. So we get this marvelous juxtaposition of opposites, birth and death, and the healing image of a woman free to be her own mediatrix in an archetypal cosmos. Here's O'Neill's final image of the pairing:

*The two make a strangely tragic picture in the wan dawn light—this big sorrowful woman hugging a haggard-faced, middle-aged drunkard against her breast, as if he were a sick child.*

*

The challenge becomes how we develop an imaginative activity so that it lives in a context that is truly animated. The key is the essentially engaging quality of the work. And for the participant in archetypal drama it is the realization that the work we do together has a value that is not some kind of limited cognitive problem-solving. It is the real work, an initiation into a creative milieu that contains the same reverberations enshrined in our most treasured art forms. And performance art (in which I include our work), blends education, the pleasure of theatrical form, the ritual aspects of an ancient devotional activity, as well as a therapeutic potency that often leads to self discovery or psychological transformation. And once these archetypal powers are tapped, they can become useful and friendly ghosts, giving back to us something of their own integrity and interest in creativity. Like Corbin's angels, our initiated creators become acquainted "with the function of 'himma,' the concentration of the heart as the organ which makes it possible to achieve a true knowledge of things." (Ibid., p. 229)

## ၍ 12 ႀ
## CONSTRUCTING THE DRAMATIC STORY

One of the early theorists of creative potential in therapy was George A. Kelly (1955) who developed what he called 'fixed role therapy' which involves the clinician's writing a narrative sketch for the client that contains a precis of a new personality, new ways to behave, and even carries a fictional name to emphasize the character differences between the person in the sketch and the client. For Kelly, unique self-experimentation, rather than healing, was at the heart of his concerns. His conviction was that no one need be trapped by their life history just because theories construe persons as entanglements of conflicting drives.

In the workshop there is a constancy of decision and action. Each protagonist is actively pursuing an imaginative destiny, a goal through which he or she will emerge in a different state. There is the sense of requisite courage, of coming up with the energy to overcome obstacles, to get to the point of self-recovery. In theatre terms, the individual is pushing hard, trying to reach that phenomenal edge where there can be a creative breakthrough. It is a quest for an alternative vision, enacting a broad sketch of possibilities, trying to come to a fresh construction of reality. And it tests the person's capacity to see imaginally, to anticipate a need for rearranging the creative field, in much the same way that a painter might paint over a space on a canvas that suddenly looks irrelevant. An emotional insight, spontaneously construed, comes into play and there is another meaning altogether, another artistic identity.

In the workshops, we go into our stories, trying to imagine what myth or god is dominant, trying to excavate the relevant issues and players of the tale. And this has its echoes in the theatre. From Bertolt Brecht (1964):

> Everything hangs on the story; it is the heart of the theatrical performance. For it is what happens *between* people that provides them with all the material they can discuss, criticize, alter. The 'story' is the theatre's greatest operation, the complete fitting together of all the gestic incidents, embracing the communications and impulses that must now go to make up the audience's entertainment. (in Willet, p. 200)

All stories honestly told have a knot of truth about them, where many strands are held together by some central core. Even if the terms and gestures are not at all times clear, there is still a momentum that ties the persons of the story together. The world is storied anew in drama, giving us a new world view, a changed occasion.

*Joe had been locked in a closet when he was young. Whenever there was psychic disturbance in his early household, his stepmother would lock him in a closet and he was told he could not cry. If he cried, the punishment would increase. We decided to recreate the conditions of this traumatic memory in the workshop. We enacted each episode. We had the mother figure, who made this demand, played by one auxiliary. Joe then created a good mother who argued the position that he was being abused. The focus was on Joe's lifelong inability to cry when he felt like crying. We had our good spirit tell him gently he could cry, that indeed he had a lot to cry about. And he was freed to move in that direction, so that tears for the first time flowed. It was a small catharsis that he had intended for a long time, and the story and the dramatic enactment allowed him to move psychically in a direction he had long repressed.*

In this dramatic exercise, the psyche of the protagonist enters both the historical conditions of a traumatic situation, but also gets the chance to change it utterly. This reminds me of a painter who is obsessed with an image that needs exploration. One thinks of Cezanne's persistent interest in particular landscape motifs in the south of France, which through consistent work he was able to transform into art. The creative act and the case history coincide. As Hillman (1983) says, in his essay on Freud:

> As depth psychology invented a new kind of practitioner and patient, a new language, a new style of ritual, and of loving, so it shaped a new genre of story, one that is neither biographical nor medical, nor confessional witness, but a narrative of the inner workings of the soul through time.... (p. 48)

And in our workshops, the actors and director become in effect historians of the soul's processes. We find a way to bring to life these buried treasures, these family stories, these poetic structures looking for voice and form. The call is ever to bring the world together, past and present, gods and men, heroes and fallen foes, the chrestomathy of incident, memory and fiction, the whole panoply of a dramatic story that goes deep enough to satisfy the soul's desire to create.

*

*The theme in this drama: dependence on a particular woman at the expense of all other activities in the person's life. The protagonist, Bob, was obsessed with Jane. He was involved with her, but she was not available enough to him. He said he wanted to dialogue with her as well as a dream figure which he identified as the Oriental Wise Woman.*

*In this drama, the protagonist played all the parts. There were no auxiliaries. The dialogues sounded like this:*

Bob. Jane, I really feel like we should spend more time together. When we're apart I think about you all the time and I'm sure we belong together.

Protagonist as Jane. Bob, you know I'm in school now and it's important for me to finish. You will get in my way if you try to see me more often than I have time for.

Bob. I know that. I want to be able to respect your time, but it's hard. I feel so drawn to you.

Director. All right. She's tied up with her work. You need to find something in you that will give you some kind of experience you think you can only get from her.

Bob. Yes. I think the Oriental Wise Woman in the dream has something to say about this. I think she knows something.

Dir. Ok. Let's put the Wise Woman in the empty chair.

Bob. I feel like there's something you know that I need to know.

Protagonist as Oriental Wise Woman. Yes. I see what you are doing. You think she can save you from all your problems: loneliness, boredom, lack of contact. But you need to find inside yourself your own way, your own path, your own individuation. You need to trust that your own story has a real value.

Bob. I know all that and yet I keep thinking if only Jane will be part of my life it will all become fine. I keep thinking over and over that without her I will fall apart.

Wise Woman. But you have an abundance inside you. I know that. You know that. But you need to keep telling the story, you need to keep reminding yourself how important those personal stories are.

Bob. I know. I know these things are in me. There's like this locked out part that keeps receding as the illusion of all this powerful beauty that comes from Jane keeps advancing.

Director. Illusion. You said illusion. Call it maya. Call it Aphrodite.

Bob. But it's just so incredibly powerful.

Dir. And what about what's inside you?

Bob. It keeps getting hammered down.

Dir. Hammered down and kept quiet.

Bob. But it's there, I can feel it. It wants expression. (To the Wise Woman) You understand expression. How do you stay concentrated on the inner thing?

Wise Woman. By activating it. By telling. By staying within the personal realms of your own understanding and knowledge. By not constantly seeking affirmation outside of you. You need to dig down into your own collective wisdom. You need to find in yourself that relational field that will feed you.

Bob. But what is this food for the soul I don't seem to find?

Wise Woman. You're close to it now. You are very close. It's not outside you. Let it guide you now.

Bob. I'm feeling very engaged in this. It feels like I'm getting the sense of what I need. And Jane is not responsible for my needs. I need to watch my own forces. There's a place in me.

Dir. Describe it.

Bob. A place of real beauty. A place of real power. It's the cornerstone of something truly wonderful. A place where the soul is alive in freedom. The soul is where the freedom begins. It's a container that is fully capable of its own extensions and its own conception of the universe.

Dir. This is the work. It is your work.

Wise Woman. It will make many things possible that seemed blocked to you.

Bob. I sense that.

The Oriental Wise Woman, in a very economical exchange, reaffirms Bob's ability to unlock creative forces: she counsels that he can live abundantly in an inner way, freed from his futile insistence that the girl friend save him.

*

> The theatre is one of the archetypal Arts of Memory, on many levels.... What is valuable about dramatic literature is that it constitutes a living record of other lives and other worlds. It is live history; and by failing to take the pains to discover the Atlantis that it represents, we turn our back on history, on the richness of culture and on the lessons of the past. *(Being An Actor,* Simon Callow)

*

*In a workshop Ken wanted to work with 'shadow material.' The work involved confrontation with a landlord who was to him the epitome of a shadow figure. Ken, a recovering addict, had recently rented an apartment. The owner, a practicing alcoholic, took Ken and his wife to dinner and proceeded to drink heavily and variously make Ken and wife very uncomfortable. We set up the opposing realities, Ken in his judgmental ego role and the landlord as the shadow figure, who also represented the angry, controlling addict that Ken once was.*

Ken. I don't like you. You're controlling, loud, ugly and you keep discounting everyone around you. I don't trust you. I can see that you don't like it that I'm not drinking with you. You keep making cracks about non-drinkers. You order a second bottle of wine.

Landlord. (Ken, reversing roles) I'm going to take care of everything. I like you. I like your wife. You tell me there's something needs fixing, it's fixed. We live and work together. You need something, I'm there for you. My word is good. Have a drink. Oh, you don't drink, I keep forgetting. Don't mind if I do. Yeah, I got a drinking problem. I can't seem to get enough of it.

Waiter, another bottle of this Chardonnario. Forget your worries. You're going to be living in my complex. Beautiful views, you name it. It's paradise and we're in this together.

Ken. I keep having visions of the Red Knight from *The Fisher King*. Did you see it? There's this furious red knight on a horse that keeps appearing as an hallucination from the subconscious of this street urchin, this bum, who has been destroyed in his relationships with people—his girlfriend was killed in a bar. Anyway, I'm really pissed at this landlord.

Director. Tell him more about what you are experiencing around him.

Ken. (To landlord) You enrage me, pal. Gordon, I can't stand being close to you. You are the most repulsive slob of a person I have ever seen. I don't want to be here anymore.

Dir. Ok, let's turn Gordon into the Shadow. Give him a dimension beyond the personal Gordon. See where this goes.

Ken. I really can't stand you. You are the darkness I can't stand to acknowledge. You make me sick. I don't want to own anything about you. You give me the creeps. But I know you're there. I know you're there, damnit! I see you in Gordon. I don't like what I see, but I see.

Shadow. (Ken, reversed) I'm a part of you. I am that energy you feel when Gordon talks. I belong to you.

Director. Ok. Let's get somebody to play the Shadow. Choose someone.

Ken selects a woman, Susan.

Dir. Ok. Now let's go back to your ego position and talk to the shadow.

Ken. I don't want to acknowledge you.

Susan. (As Shadow) I am already in you. I need to be felt for what I am. I am not you. I need to be experienced for what I am. I think you don't want to let me have any existence because I remind you of things you want to remove from your life. I understand that. But remember that I have useful things for you as well. I have instinct, I have power. I am very powerful.

Ken. (Eyes closed) I know that. And yet. (Pause) There's something about you I don't know how to deal with. I thought I got rid of you. I had all that denial for so long. Now I don't have a place for you. You are part of my past.

Susan. (Shadow) No, I'm here now. I'm still here. But you don't need to use me to destroy you. You can take me for what I'm worth. I'm also a gift in your inner life. I'm a force that can give your spiritual energy strength.

Ken. I know. I have to let you come in. I don't want you to always have to live out there. Somebody else has these problems, dark sides. I need you too. You are part of me.

Dir. (To Shadow) Reach out to him.

Susan. (Shadow) Take me back. Take what I can give you back. I can be an important part of you.

Ken. (Reaching out) I do take you back. I welcome you as part of me. I'll try to find a place for you. I'll try to see what I'm doing with you.

Ken had re-visioned the shadow, giving it a substantial place that heretofore had been denied to it. He came to terms with this energy that had once been so dominant in an altogether destructive way. He had been possessed by his projected shadow and had fought hard to remove its effects on him. (Of course, living in a shadow character's 'complex' is bound to have a substantial effect on a protagonist.) By working with this material, Ken developed another way of seeing his life and the tendency to both repress and project the shadow. This made him constantly guarded against anyone who provided a hook for this repressed force. By seeing that this was an inner content, he was able to begin working with shadow material, recognizing the archetypal basis for much of his personalized agony with the landlord. This proved to be helpful to him.

## ℘ 13 ☙

## ARTAUD, YEATS AND THE ALCHEMICAL THEATRE

*There is a mysterious identity of essence between the principle of theater and that of alchemy. For like alchemy, the theater, considered from the point of view of its deepest principle, is developed from a certain number of fundamentals which are the same for all the arts and which aim on the spiritual and imaginary level at an efficacy analogous to the process which in the physical world actually turns all matter into gold. (The Theatre and Its Double,* Antonin Artaud)

The relationship between theatre and alchemy is an old one. Both are forms of art which embody forces of transformation. As Jung remarked in *Psychology and Alchemy* (CW 12, p. 482): "Not for nothing did alchemy style itself an 'art,' feeling—and rightly so—that it was concerned with creative processes that can be truly grasped only by experience, though intellect may give them a name." In a parallel light in theatre history, Ben Jonson's play *The Alchemist* (1610) explores the curious symbolic realm in which alchemy and characters of theatrical/alchemical device interact on stage. As Antonin Artaud (1896-1948) says: "All true alchemists know that the alchemical symbol is a mirage as the theater is a mirage." (*Double*, p. 49)

Artaud, perhaps more than any other theorist of the twentieth century, was concerned with finding the root mystery and cause of theatrical activity. A revolutionary thinker and extraordinary actor/director in France in the 1920s and 30s, he co-founded the Theatre Jarry, where he produced several plays, including his own, *The Cenci* (1935) which exhibited many of his theories. His seminal book *The Theatre and Its Double* (1958) describes theatrical modes that later become identifying traits of various theatrical movements, including the theatre of the absurd and ritual theatre. Artaud's theatre conceptions involved a movement toward a ritual vitality that tapped ancient energies and this is much in keeping with our attempts in the archetypal drama workshops. We want to find the essence of drama, return to its rigorous origins and allow the entire mental and physical being to enter an expansive, archetypal realm in which images and sound are alive. Artaud, again:

> I believe that the Mysteries of Eleusis must have consisted of projections and precipitations of conflicts, indescribable battles of principles... resolved by conjunctions unimaginably strange to our waking minds, dissolving all appearances into one unique expression which must have been the equivalent of spiritualized gold. (Ibid., p. 52)

And so it happens in theatrical expression when there is a complete resolution of some kind of major operative conflict. It might be added that the peace that sometimes prevails at the end of tragedy echoes these concerns.

One thinks of Emily Dickinson's "After great pain/ A formal feeling comes...." We are talking about confronting the deepest mysteries of the inner life of man & woman, and the challenge as ever is to find the right imaginative mix, the alchemical energy formed perhaps of that capacity for astonishment and clarity that is at the heart of the best dramatic efforts.

*In the workshop exercise, she said she wanted to dialogue with two essential parts of her nature and she called one the 'magenta' or artistic side and the other was the 'beige' or conformist side. We cast the two sides and she said that behind the beige side was what she referred to as Formula Female and we cast her. She said that 'Formula Female' had all the prescriptions for successful activity in the corporate and work world. She knew exactly how to dress, wear makeup and carry herself. She had nothing but unkind things to say to this figure although she acknowledged that she had her place, though her dominance made it tough to really care much for her. The side of her that was construed as artistic in nature had a strenuous dialogue with Formula Female, and the 'Magenta' side of her psyche resolved to make more time to pursue artistic aims. In the sharing that followed the dramatic event, there was much discussion about power, the patriarchy and different ideas about 'the norm' as it gets practiced in most job situations.*

*

On what does the imagination thrive? There seem to be some answers in our discussion, though the process of creating powerful spontaneous drama will I think often depend on a vast variety of elements that come together to form it. What do we seek in this kind of work? Let me go back to Artaud:

> It is certain that we need above all a theater that wakes us up: nerves and heart.... Our long habit of seeking diversion has made us forget the idea of a serious theater, which, overturning our preconceptions, inspires us with the fiery magnetism of its images and acts upon us like a spiritual therapeutics whose touch can never be forgotten. (Ibid., p. 85)

In the irony that made him the unique poet and actor that he was, Artaud called his declarations The Theater of Cruelty, defining cruelty as "a cosmic rigor and implacable necessity, in the gnostic sense of a living whirlwind that devours the darkness, in the sense of that pain apart from whose ineluctable necessity life could not continue...." (Ibid., p. 102)

And W.B. Yeats (1865-1939) found this same kind of paradoxical intensity in his own discoveries in the realms of art:

> As life goes on we discover that certain thoughts sustain us in defeat, or give us victory, whether over ourselves or others, and it is these

> thoughts, tested by passion, that we call convictions.... We begin to live when we have conceived life as tragedy. *(Autobiography,* p. 189)

Yeats in his dramatic work was interested in what he called 'tragic ecstasy.' What he was after was a mood that awakened the mind to deeply poetic states. There was in Yeats a mystical faith in the power of dramatic expression. He held fast to it through the vicissitudes of attempts to create a National Irish Theatre, his disappointments around his proposed marital union with Maud Gonne and the public rejection of his mystical vision in plays like *The Countess Cathleen.* In a moving passage of his memoir called *Explorations,* we get this plea: "I wanted a theatre where the greatest passion and all the permanent interests of men might be displayed that we might find them not alone over a book but, as I said again and again, lover by lover, friend by friend. All I wanted was impossible and I wore out my youth in its pursuit, but now I know it is the mystery to come." (p. 313)

Herein I feel a tremendous kinship with Yeats' quest. At times I feel what we are doing in our workshops is a continuation of this idea of a place where 'passion and permanent interests' might be played out in a way that cannot happen in the commercial theatre as we now know it. I too have worn out some of my youth in this pursuit and I've seen others do the same. But the form of our work provides a way to rehabilitate the art of theatre, to return soul to theatre. There is a deep paradox here, an irony that does not come to a quick finish. It is that we are involved in mysteries when we are doing our drama work and the mystery gets played out at various levels. We enter the archetypal theatre and our discoveries are in a depth of exploratory experience that produces an enigmatic satisfaction and gratitude. There is a guiding presence that might involve the myth of Dionysus, in all his pandemonium and ecstasy. Dionysus was the god of tragic contrast and double birth, born of both heaven and earth. The inner force of his dual nature was so great that he appeared among men like an overwhelming storm. In our revitalized spontaneous theatre, great contrasting forces are kept alive and ready to pour forth renewing artistic energy.

*

Archetypal figures peopled Yeats's life and work: the characters of the plays, the Sages and Wizards, but also the persons of his life, childhood idol and actor Henry Irving, anima figure Maud Gonne, loyal great mother Mrs. Yeats and so on. We can fairly say that Yeats lived a passionate poetic life and found in the dramatic imagination something in which his spirit could enter and often thrive. Andrew Parkin (1978) argues that Yeats's view of the imagination is in the Platonic and Neoplatonic traditions "owing much to Blake, Coleridge and Wordsworth."

> The supreme test of the modern imagination for Yeats is to make imagination itself sacred; hence the mystical order he forms and his experiments with symbols....All images and impulses from the imagination, Yeats believed, could likewise be made sacred in the modern age by shaping and ordering them 'in beauty and in peace' through association 'deliberately'...and directly with the history of the soul.... (p. 18)

It is the rediscovery of the sacred in our dramatic enactments that actualizes the joy in creation that the work deeply embodies. Experience has shown that the spontaneous drama is capable of manifesting numinous figures and giving them language and palpable imaginal form. It harks back to the imagination's ability to perceive the essential mystery at the heart of existence, especially when it is an embodied vision that is presented in dialogue and symbolic enactment. The coherence that comes alive in our workshops emerges from a sometimes mystical opening of communal theatrical life that embraces the soul's manifest desire to create just the right particulars.

*Marla chose as her historical character Georgia O'Keefe and she began talking about her, what she meant to her and she decided to talk with her at her New Mexico home at Abiquiu and we arranged the stage for her. She picked another woman to play the part of Georgia and then ensued her archetypal drama in which we saw Georgia embodied by another. Marla asked Georgia about her life in New York with Alfred Stieglitz and what that meant to her and about her decision to move to New Mexico to continue her destiny without him. Georgia simply said that her relationship with Stieglitz was important to her but that it was also important that she move to New Mexico to continue her life. She did not express much sadness about any decision in her life. It was all a story of her own personal progress and quest. Those of us witnessing this work I believe simultaneously had the deepest sense that we were witnessing not just a simulacrum of this event, but something much more profound. It seemed as though Marla had actually contacted Georgia O'Keefe and that the woman chosen to play Georgia had entered her sensibility in such a complete way that there was no distance between the fictional and the actual realms. The souls of Marla and Georgia O'Keefe were in some kind of communion and a deeply sacred imaginative movement was occurring right before us. At the end, we asked questions of both of them in role. They were also moved by the authenticity of their contact. In the end, we formed a circle around them both and thanked them for their illuminating discourse.*

Which in some sense brings us back to Yeats's idea of *Anima Mundi*, the universal container of memories, images and emotional force fields which our individual imaginations can reach through symbolic and visionary realms. And something truly great comes about in these moments—a joy, to be sure, but also a complex understanding of this capacity we have for a spiritual quest that takes us into new regions of rigorous vitality. Imagination is herein triggered by intense emotion and the desire to enter a sphere of the historically creative that has long been associated with art and myth. It is the search for beatific vision, which is propelled by a healing flow of imaginative energy. And in this quest, the symbolic personages in our archetypal dramas allow us to experience this transformative region in which the imaginative is given a chance to be heard and recognized in its full profusion.

*

Archetypal drama inspires the very fabric of our beings and gives us a place on which we can operate and find our truest natures. The alchemical theatre calls us to be something deeper; it is a manifestation of the dark and numinous forces within us that can arrive at another form of destiny, a field in which we are alive with new knowledge, new energies, and a task that calls us into action.

## ꧁ 14 ꧂
## WORKING MOMENTUM

*Every dialogue that pushes forward into territory hedged about by fear and resistance is aiming at something vital, and by impelling the one partner to integrate his wholeness it forces the other to take up a broader position. He too is impelled toward wholeness, for without this he would not be able to push the dialogue deeper and deeper into those fear-bound regions.* (Jung, CW 8, p. 102 )

In the following archetypal drama, the dichotomy between two powerful internalized forces was the subject. Kim (the protagonist) called them 'the cynic' and the 'dreamer' at first, but on beginning the drama, the polarities became 'the ice queen' and 'the soft woman.' As she began moving back and forth between the two forms, it became clear that we had a strong oppositional field established.

Ice Queen. I'm in control here. I don't want to put up with any bullshit. I don't want to hear anything about all this mamby pamby granola and sunshine bullshit. I'm into total war and I have the power to destroy you.
Soft Woman. (wearing a blanket) I don't know what to say to you. You're so angry. I'm afraid of you.
Ice Queen. You had better be afraid of me. I'm a great power. You dumb worthless idiot!
Soft Woman. What do you want to do to me?
Ice Queen. I'm going to eat you alive.

This kind of exchange went on for quite a while. She then cast a male auxiliary first as the soft woman, then another male as the ice queen. The choices of male helpers seemed to me to underscore her desire for a certain kind of volatile masculine edge to the piece. I knew there was another archetypal element in the ice queen's energy.

Director. What is the force behind the ice queen?
Kim. Rage.
Dir. Ok. Let's cast rage.

She then casts another male to play Rage, and entangles them, with Rage behind the Ice Queen, holding her in a hammer lock. The exchanges between the Ice Queen and the soft woman continue at a heated pace.

I was convinced there was a counter-force involved in the soft woman's world as well.

Dir. What's the force behind the soft woman's world?

Kim. I was hoping you wouldn't ask. It's weakness.
Dir. Right. Ok. Let's cast weakness.
Kim. I don't want to cast weakness! (Pause) Oh, all right. (She picks a woman) She needs to be down here on the ground next to me.
Dir. How would you feel about reversing roles with Weakness?
Kim (loud) I won't do weakness! I won't! I don't want to play weakness!
Dir. Ok. Fine. But there she is. Cling to her, Weakness.
Kim. I can't stand it. You poor feeble little thing!

And with her companion (cast earlier) all the figures continue conversing with Ice Queen/Rage. I ask Kim if there is the sense of a larger figure that could complete the drama and Kim decides it must be some form of The Feminine Archetype. She casts a woman.

The Feminine. I can show you strength. I can inspire a whole realm of power and integrity.
Kim. I don't believe you. You have let me down too often. You're nothing but a bunch of weakness. You're phony and weak.
Ice Queen. Don't you do it. Don't even think of it. If you let go of me, I'll kill you. You miserable idiot!
The Feminine. There's strength in weakness.
Kim. How do I know that?

We then add another pole to the Feminine, a negative Kali-like joining element, which I had stand back to back with the original figure.

Negative Feminine. I have all the power in the world.
Kim. Do you have snakes?
Neg. Fem. Yes.
Kim. Do you have arrows and swords and artillery?
Neg. Fem. Yes, everything you need to be destructive.
The Feminine. (revolving) We're part of you. We don't have to become like Ice Queen. You can make a life with us. And you can live without destruction.
Kim. How do I know that?
The Feminine. Trust me. I am on your side. I want you to be complete. Follow me.

Kim then joins the Feminine with her Double and Weakness. They embrace, the five of them forming a sort of whole. Ice Queen still grunts and threatens. Kim then goes to Ice Queen/Rage and reluctantly embraces them. Then a long embrace with Kim & Ice Queen and a kind of defusing occurs. She then de-roles all the players. We then form a support circle and the group gives her feedback.

Dir. How are you?

Kim. I felt I was hearing myself from all these different voices. It felt like the whole thing was going on inside my being.

Various voices. This was really powerful...I was glad you did that...I felt it was about something I'm going through...I was reminded of St. Paul's experience in Corinthians when the voice of God says 'My strength will be made perfect in your weakness.' Freud talked about love and death, Eros and Thanatos. Rage and destruction and shadow elements are such a part of our history...We have always been attracted to our destructive tendencies. It's only by positing and trusting a counterforce that we begin finding another dimension that can sustain us. This becomes an inward movement, an attempt to be aware of antinomies or opposites that must do battle on a personal level in the heart of each individual...I know Ice Queen really well...I'm really thankful you did this work, Kim...That energy of the Ice Queen is sometimes so strong...But there are other elements that have strength too....

*

## SESSION. *THE BIG WOUND STRIKES BACK*

The protagonist, Mel, chooses a companion, an inner alter-ego.

Director. What do you want to deal with?

Mel as Protagonist. There's this awfulness that keeps getting at me. Keeps getting into my head, my shoulders, makes my eyes twitch. Some old ugly awful senex. I call him Crud.

Dir. How do you want to meet with him.

Mel. I need to tell him off first. You asshole, you hateful scumbucket.

Mel then takes two chairs, puts one on top of another, one tilting. He then takes the chair he's sitting on and throws it into the other chairs.

Dir. What's next?

Mel. That feels good. I took him down. Ah. (Pause) Next, my father, Don.

Dir. Present Don.

Protagonist as Don. I'm Don, I run this ranch. Hello Mel. (to Dir.) He doesn't say much.

Dir. Reverse roles. Back to your own. Speak to him.

Mel. You won't talk about this, you never talk about this.

Dir. He won't talk. Who else do you need to talk to.

Mel. My grandmother. She's where the anger started.

Dir. Present grandmother.

Protagonist as Grandmother. I'm Melba. I run this family. I get what I want when I want it. I own the whole damn property.
Dir. What's behind these people? What keeps them going?
Prot. Denial and Rage.
Dir. Cast Denial and Rage.

Two others named and cast. Protagonist presents Denial & Rage.

Denial. I'm Denial. I don't make waves. I have my own way of doing things. I read *People Magazine.*
Rage. I'm Rage. I'm powerful. I run this family. I was responsible for the suicide of one family member. Nothing gets in my way.
Dir. Talk to grandmother.
Mel. I hate you grandma. You ruined my father. You ruined the ranch. You caused a suicide. I hate you.
Grandma. (Prot. in reversed role) Na na na na. I don't listen to you. (exit)
Mel. She wouldn't listen to anything like that.

Dir. Talk to your inner self.
Mel. What should we do now?
Companion. What do you think?
Mel. There's something behind this.
Companion. What's behind this?
Mel. A big wound.
Dir. A big wound behind?
Mel. Denial and Rage.
Dir. Let's cast the Big Wound.
Mel. I don't know who to cast. (Pause) Tom.

Tom enters.

Dir. Ok. Let's have you present Big Wound.
Protagonist as Big Wound. I'm the big bleeding blue wound. I hurt. I always hurt. I hurt here in the stomach, and in the head, and I just don't stop hurting. It's awful. I need something, someone. I can't take this.
Dir. (to Tom) Ok. Repeat as much of that as you can remember.

Tom does this.

Denial. You don't need anything. I'll take care of everything.
Rage. All this pisses me off.
Dir. Ok. What else do you need here? Where's the healing force?
Mel. The Magician.

Dir. Ok. Let's bring the magician out.

Mel. Johnny.

Johnny. (as Magician) I'm the magician. I can help you put this together. I can sew this thing up and give you the bow. I can help you deal with the wound.

Mel. I know you can.

Dir. How's this now?

Mel. (straining) There's something else here. Striving. Social Striving.

Dir. We need Striving. Let's cast it.

Mel. Pete.

Pete. (as Striving) I'm your upward mobility. You don't need all this inner bullshit. What is all this? You need to get up the social and corporate ladder. You need to make it big. Forget all this.

Mel. But....but....yeah, I know all that.

Dir. Talk to your inner self.

Mel. I hear this guy.

Dir. (Prompting Big Wound) But I need you.

Big Wound. But I need you. I'm hurting.

Dir. Why not take the Big Wound away from Denial and Rage.

Big Wound. Take me away.

Denial and Rage. Don't make a move. You're safe here.

Mel takes Big Wound away from behind Denial and Rage & over to his companion. Striving is behind them.

Big Wound. I need you to open your heart.

Mel. I know you do.

Companion. I'm afraid.

Mel. I am. I need to try to be creative. I need to figure this out.

Companion. Yes, you do.

Dir. Is there a creative force available to you?

Mel. We'll get to that. I need to talk to the Wound. (to Wound) I know you were damaged. They sent you to that terrible pre-school. They didn't want you around. And all that silent hatred and denial. All that tension. (Grabbing his head) They hurt you and they didn't even know it.

Big Wound. I need you Mel.

Mel. I know. We need something else now. The Creative Angel.

Dir. The Creative Angel. Cast it.

Mel. Fran.

Protagonist as Creative Angel. I'm your creative angel. I can be creative with the most awful problems. I can help you find your way.

Fran. (as Creative Angel) I can be creative with the most awful problems. I can help you find your way.
Dir. What do you need to do now?
Mel. Deal with the wound. (To Wound) Take care of you.

He embraces the Big Wound.
He then embraces himself as the Companion.
Creative Angel and Striving join in.

*

This felt like a completed archetypal drama. It had beginning personal elements and then the archetypal entities began to predominate. The protagonist found an answer to his symptomatic self-condemnation and anger. He saw that the family structure had never allowed much movement of emotion and he saw how the badly damaged Big Wound from childhood continued to need his attention. He saw through his malaise to a creative response that actualized in him progressive forces that came to his aid. As the piece approached a closing, Mel took charge, becoming a fierce dramatic worker. His reaction to the Director—"We'll get to that"—was spoken with great force; he had entered his own range of concerns and his own sense of timing.

From the Protagonist: "In summary the knowledge I gained from all this was: 1. Rage and Denial are not people but defenses. 2. The Wounded Child is the Magician. 3. I have a Wounded Child. 4. There are angels. 5. I can cry and it feels good to feel."

*

At times there is a blessedness in the air when persons are encountering deep experience and giving it dramatic form. Something comes to light, eyes make contact with eyes, and there is a descent into a space that can be named an inner darkness brought to light in these forms, but it is truly refreshing to head that way, to bring one's luggage and privacy into the primordial regions where the archetypes collide and play their own music. One thinks it was meant to be like this, creative and mild, deadly serious and yet playful beyond imagining. It is the body finding a place to position the psyche; it reaches through paradox to land in space that matters ever so deeply. We who were out in the diminished land of isolation and questions with no reply suddenly find voices and a ceremonial entrance that welcomes us and hands us back our rights as creators and emotionally charged beings with purpose and power and plenty. An abundance is born of the heart's driving ambition to find fields on which to play, to get to the scene just unfolding at the dramatic threshold where each participant is given a deepened self knowledge involving manifold energies.

*

## SESSION. *A QUATERNITY ARISES: FEAR OF DYING*

When Ann began dialoguing with the death she feared so much, it became clear that she was really talking about two forms of death, one that was the gateway to eternal life, the other a finality that was the end of all existence for her. Behind these forms, there stood doubt and faith. We cast all four of these entities.

Ann. I want you with me.
Open Death. I am death that is not death. I will lead you to eternal life.
Ann. Oh, I want to believe in you. (to Closed Death) But you, you want to take everything away. You want to end everything.
Closed Death. I am the end of all. Nothing follows me.
Doubt. I don't know what to believe. One day one thing one day another. I keep you in a state of confusion.
Faith. I give you the will to stay on the path. You are going to heaven. You must trust in the goodness of God.

**Faith**

|

**Open—** DEATH **—Closed**

|

**Doubt**

This formed a kind of quaternity and we seated everyone in chairs, back to back. We then turned to the disease Ann was struggling with, which she first presented and then we cast.

Protagonist as Disease. I am Lupus Erythematosus. I am an inflammatory connective tissue disorder of unknown etiology. I attack your joints and I am unpredictable. I may go into remission and stay or I may flare up and bring you great misery.
Dir. There's an anger attached to this, isn't there.
Ann. Yes, a great rage that I should have to go through this.
Dir. Present the anger.
Protagonist as Anger. I hate you, Lupus. I hate what you are doing to me. I want to live to see my children grow up, and my grandchildren.
Dir. What is it you seek in all this?
Ann. Peace of Mind.

Dir. Ok. Let's cast as peace of mind. Present it.

Protagonist as Peace of Mind. I'm your peace of mind. I want you to have some ease. I don't want you to suffer.

Dir. What's the other side of peace of mind?

Ann. I think it's weakness.

Dir. Let's present and cast weakness.

Pt. as Weakness. I'm what's weak in you. I can't stand up to any of this. It's all too much. I don't have the strength for it.

Dir. So these are in opposition—peace and weakness.

Ann. Yes.

Dir. So let's put them back to back and have them revolve.

(Weakness and Peace of Mind slowly revolve, each speaking its point of view as it confronts Ann)

Dir. What can help you deal with this? What's missing here?

Ann. A father figure. My father when he was there for me. No, a larger father, a father figure.

Dir. A father figure. Ok. Let's have the father figure. Present him.

Protagonist as Father Figure. I'm the father. I helped you through tough times. Remember how it was when your mother was ill. I took your hand and we dealt with it. I always knew you were strong.

(Ann casts the figure and there is an exchange.)

Ann. I knew your strength would get me through this. I could count on you.

Father Figure. I'm still with you. You just have to ask me and I'll be there for you.

Ann. I know that. I trust you.

Dir. Now Father Figure, why don't you take Ann (and her companion) on a tour of her world. Just take her by the hand and lead her around. And all you various players, please speak to her in character as she goes around you.

(A cacophony of voices from all the figures as Ann and her father figure encircle the others.)

Dir. How is that?

Ann. Good. It feels complete.

Dir. Yes. Now de-role everyone and—if you like—speak to each character.

(She does this, slowly de-roling everyone and speaking to their role, giving each a hug and thanks. De-roling allows participants to return to their own states of being, not unlike what an actor goes through after a performance, removing makeup and returning to the non-theatrical world.)

We then formed a circle for brief sharing, took a break, and then began a somewhat lengthy formal sharing.

Various voices. Ann, I want to thank you for your work. It took a lot of courage to go into this material. I felt your grief and strength all the way.... I just want to say I've been struggling with a threatening physical problem—not the same one—but I feel clearer about what I have to do.... The same sense of weakness keeps happening to me. I'm glad you did this. It opened a lot of issues.... Yes, I'd like to thank you for looking at so many sides of this. It would have been simple to stay on the positive side. But you were willing to face the ambivalence and the complexity.... I'm really touched.

Ann. Thank you all for helping me.

Dir. This felt like something very complete.

Ann. Yes. I'm exhausted. But it does feel complete.

Dir. You see Jung had this idea of wholeness, of completeness he called individuation. I think your work had something to do with a complete story. A shared enactment that involved all of us. And there is the sense of having brought your current life struggle to some imaginative and emotional resolution. I was glad to be part of it.

Ann. I'm grateful for the chance to go into it. It feels like a gift.

Dir. For all of us.

## ꧁ 15 ꧂
# MOBILIZATION OF THE NUMINOUS

*Holiness means that an idea or thing possesses the highest value.... Holiness is also revelatory: It is the illuminative power emanating from an archetypal figure.* (CW 11, p. 152)

In our work, there is the effort to keep the numinous realms alive. We want to experience the complexity and sovereignty of the sacred, putting us into a context that will explore the holiness of our psychic capacities. The production of numinous figures often proceeds from the interaction of opposites. In the two archetypal dramas that follow, the capacity of the drama to explore themes dense with numinous potential is given a strong position on our stage.

*

## THE DRAMATIC SAGA OF BREATH

Eleanor, a hospitalized patient who suffered from post-traumatic problems and depression, wanted to create a drama around the issue of hopelessness. We talked of her severe depressions and frequent suicide attempts. We first had her present the character of Hopelessness:

Protagonist as Hopelessness. I try to keep going but there is nothing but hopelessness. I don't think I can go on. I'm so huge. Hopelessness is so huge. But I don't want to give Suicide the chance to end this in such a small way.

Director. We need to cast Suicide.

Pt. Yes.

Dir. Present Suicide.

Protagonist as Suicide. I can put an end to this suffering. I'm a quick practical solution.

Co-Director (Auxiliary) as Hopelessness. I'm too big. I'm vast and I don't want you taking over and ending me before my time. You just want to reduce what I am.

Dir. Do we need Hope here as well?

Pt. Yes.

Dir. Present Hope.

Protagonist as Hope. I'm the hope you need to go on. I am here to push you on, to give you strength.

Auxiliary as Suicide. I'm efficient and I give you the choice of going no further.

Auxiliary as Hopelessness. I don't want to go your tiny way. I'm too big.

Aux. as Suicide. You are much too big. That's the problem.

Here the Protagonist began sobbing and the Co-Director began suggesting she breathe into it.

Co-Dir. Breathe. Let breath come on its own. Breathe into it. (Pt. & Co-Dir. begin deep breathing together.)
Dir. Let's cast Breath. (A chair is brought out facing Hope and Hopelessness. A patient is cast to play Hopelessness.)
Protagonist as Breath. I'm your Breath. I bring you life. I'm the spirit of life. I do what comes naturally to maintain your life.
Aux. as Hopelessness. It's too hard. I hear you but I don't know if I can go on.
Pt. as Breath. You have to because you need to keep living. Follow my lead.
Co-Dir. Breathe with her. Hopelessness, breathe with her.
Pt. as Breath. Yes, follow me. Let me lead you.
Aux. as Hopelessness. I'll try.

For the next few minutes, there is a real effort amid great emotion to follow the lead of Breath in a kind of birth of breath process that brings into play the whole emotional arena of a struggle for life.

> **Breath becomes Spirit and goes deep into the elemental process here, the waking deluge of the struggle for life continues vehemently and there is a sense of real power. Hopelessness is overwhelmed in the energetic uplift and Suicide is pushed away by Hopelessness who becomes a kind of echo or resonator of Breath's lead. There occurs here a sudden emotional surge that fills the entire room with an expansive and numinous force.**

In the context explored here, there was a form of knowledge enacted that transcends mere counseling or therapy; there is the release from suffering that is reminiscent of soul retrieval as practiced in numerous shamanic ceremonies. There is what Jung would call an archetypal experience that is born of the mystery and miracle of transformative energy. It is not a matter of information, but the internalization (and extension in dramatic form) of deep emotional power. And there is an opposition set up that has about it a tension that is extraordinarily palpable. Life and death, hopelessness and breath find an intrinsic enantiodromia (or a running counter to) that becomes the specific counterforce that this person needs to continue her own life's journey.

## HISTORICAL TRAUMA

Mona, a Lakota Sioux woman, entered our dramatic stage with the simple suggestion that her piece be about Historical Trauma. During the group check-in, Mona talked deeply about the plight of her people, The Lakotas, and she asked about enacting a drama about her people's history.

Her original character was Historical Trauma which she presented:

Protagonist as Historical Trauma. We have suffered great pain and we had our language taken from us. We were sent to boarding schools and we were treated severely by the US Government.

She then created a character called Wounded Knee:

Protagonist as Wounded Knee. Because gold was found here I became a target. There was a treaty broken here. There was fighting and killing.

She then presented the US Government:

Protagonist as US Government. We did what we had to do in terms of our expansion. We could have made things even worse for you. We may have been harsh, but we had our business to attend to.

The Director then asked Mona to present the forces behind Historical Trauma that made up the suffering of her people.

Protagonist. They are Alcoholism, Sexual Abuse, Boarding School and Loss of Language.

She cast persons from the group and stood behind them and presented each element.

Protagonist as Alcoholism. I am made up of despair. I take this drug in order to forget. I kill off our people in great numbers.

Protagonist as Sexual Abuse. I was present in all the dislocations and the boarding schools. I was the dirty secret that went on all the time.

Protagonist as Boarding School. I was taken away from my land and my strength. I was given this awful fate. I was put away. This was a prison and it destroyed our spirits.

Protagonist as Loss of Language. My language was important to my people. We had to learn English and be what we were not. It was another form of disintegration and shaming.

The Director then asked Mona what was next in this story.

Mona. We need the forces that make up our people. They are Ancestors and the Land and the Great Spirit.

Director. What I'd like you to do is pick persons from the group to represent those forces and then stand behind them and inform them.

Protagonist as Ancestors. We have been here a long time. We fought for our way of life. We have suffered through all the anguish. We wanted our way of life to continue to flourish.

Protagonist as Land. I am what made you whole. I was the living thing on which the people were able to prosper. I was the ground of your sustenance.

Protagonist as Great Spirit. I gave you clarity and strength. I was your light and your power when there was difficulty. I am with you always.

The Director and Mona walked around the circle and we talked of what more needed to be added. We talked about whether the American People was different from the US Government. She decided to create a character called the American People:

Protagonist as American People. I need to learn from you. Yours is a story that goes far back into the history of this continent.

The Director and Mona then walked around and she listened to the cast of characters and sometimes interacted with them. We then had them all speak ensemble, so that there was a great deal of sound in the room. We then talked of how this piece of work could be concluded. Mona mentioned the place of the Storyteller, cast it, and Mona presented it while moving around the already cast characters, who were now speaking in character simultaneously:

Protagonist as Storyteller. I will remember these stories. These stories tell a tale of suffering, but also of strength and courage. These stories are our stories and they will not leave us. I will tell of our land and our ancestors and the Great Spirit. I will tell of Wounded Knee and the awful happenings in the boarding schools. It will not be forgotten. It will live with our people forever, and these stories will form a living legacy for our people.

In the closing, the remainder of the group formed a circle around the inner circle of characters. Mona joined the outer circle and introduced a song to the group and the entire group joined in the song. There was a great deal of weeping, fervor and emotional closeness. There was the sense of having entered a deeply pivotal archetypal process that was born of historical trauma and the capacity of the piece to spontaneously generate dramatic energy to contain the powerful story. There was a great fullness in the silence after the piece closed. The sharing was rich and full of supportive and generously articulated feeling. We had all been transported to another level of intensity by Mona's deep creation and there was a gratitude that we had shared the journey together.

## ꕥ 16 ꕥ
## A CURTAIN CALL, A BOW AND AN EXIT

*I should like to hand it over to a profession which does not yet exist, a profession of LAY curers of souls who need not be doctors and should not be priests.* (Freud, to Pfister, 25Novl928)

*When the spontaneous dialogues of thought are approached from this point of view, they flower into drama, poetry, prayer.* (*Invisible Guests*, Mary Watkins)

An important feature of this work for me is the extent to which one reaches a state of completeness and rest. It is as though the dramatic movements contain within them a demand that the psychic/physical aspects of the human being process an entire emotional/imaginal world and then wind down from it and find closure and repose in a way that is remarkably similar to the course of a play with its exposition, rising action, climax, anti-climax and then the various resolutions and reconciliations toward the last act. Exhausted, pleased, spent, rejuvenated, rejoicing in work well done, the players take their curtain calls and later clasp hands or embrace and exit the great stage. Various forms of personal, familial and archetypal fate were staged and explored and now one is slightly removed from the demands of the drama, where great forces struggled for understanding or power or love.

*

What are we attempting in our work is intimately connected with dialogue as a way of enlarging human understanding. Experience has shown that creative dialogue translates participants into a refreshing community where language mediates rapport at new levels of understanding. Jung speaks of the dialogue in a way that moves our argument along:

> The present day shows with appalling clarity how little able people are to let the other man's argument count, although this capacity is a fundamental and indispensable condition for any human community.... For, to the degree that he does not admit the validity of the other person, he denies the 'other' within himself the right to exist—and vice versa. The capacity for inner dialogue is a touchstone for outer objectivity. *(The Transcendent Function,* CW 8, pp. 89-90)

The courage to explore one's own depth is a recurring theme in the archetypal drama workshops. The work plunges the psyche down into the uncertainty of inner forces, where one encounters foreign entities that have their own forms of discourse and image. It is often demanding. It calls for strength. Often, a person entering this territory feels a certain knot in the stomach, there is an imploding that is not immediately nameable. One says:

"I have this feeling, this sense of something disturbing begging to make itself known. I don't really have a name for it." The experimental conjoining that goes on in our dramatic work parallels Jung's ideas on the advantages of getting into relationship with oppositional forces, bringing in a generated tension and finding a resolution.

In our archetypal dramatic work, the inner world is not just talked about, but given stage and scene, prop and dimension. We make dramatic events and they give back something of ourselves clothed in metaphor. There is a shifting and commingling of complex and archetype, so that the world of the personal and the transpersonal (archetypal) are moving simultaneously toward creative events. Jung, again:

> One of the greatest obstacles to psychological understanding is the inquisitive desire to know whether the psychological factor adduced is 'true' or 'correct'.... Equally childish is the prejudice against the role which mythological assumptions play in the life of the psyche.... Mythologems exist even though their statements do not coincide with our incommensurable idea of 'truth.' (CW 8, p. 91)

A need for suspension of disbelief calls to us here, a need to allow into imaginal existence the passionate reveries of the soul's secret life. It is no small task. To be in psyche, to be able to get to those connecting forces that align us with the depths of psychological being may be our greatest challenge. Jung's concluding paragraph in this seminal essay could serve as an inducement to all those who wonder about the value of therapeutic work that includes a dramatic confrontation with inner oppositional figures:

> As the process of coming to terms with the counter-position has a total character, nothing is excluded. Everything takes part in the discussion, even if only fragments become conscious. Consciousness is continually widened through confrontation with previously unconscious contents...Where the necessary premises exist, the transcendent function...is a way of attaining liberation by one's own efforts and of finding the courage to be oneself. (Ibid., p. 91)

And the process of coming to terms with the psyche turns on understanding the fictive and the multiple as opposed to the 'real' and 'the one.' Mary Watkins (1986) in *Invisible Guests* gets deeply into this: "Each imaginal figure provides a different perspective through which events and the self can be viewed. We readily acknowledge the virtue of multiplicity in literature and drama...." (p. 106)

The recurring theme in Jung is toward individuation, of finding one's own path. And this involves the courage to become conscious of one's solitary reflective existence. This has affirmations in many theatre contexts where the director is a kind of midwife bringing the play and the individual actor to a new birth. The parallel in archetypal drama workshops is that the director often takes on the archetypal role of a magus who guides the other players into deep aspects of dramatic and psychic life. Here the language can sound religious and often becomes so in the performance theories of Grotowski and Brook. Victor Turner (1982), in *From Ritual to Theatre,* makes a valuable contribution to our discussion:

> And when we act on the stage, whatever our stage may be, we must now in this reflexive age of psychoanalysis and semiotics as never before, bring into the symbolic or fictitious world the urgent problems of our reality. We have to go into the subjunctive world of monsters, demons, and clowns, of cruelty and poetry, in order to make sense of our daily lives, earning our daily bread. (p. 122)

After leading many intensive courses and workshops in archetypal drama I now know things about this work that were inaccessible before. The work continually surprises, inspires and gives coherent ideas about the process of imaginative construction. The invention that makes the work a marvel moves in various orbits and includes prayerfulness, grandeur, minute particularity and the dwelling of human beings in sacred space. It has its own energy and parameters and it does not bend to the conscious will, but weaves its story from the actual archetypal forces that are awakened when the action progresses. Here are reports on classes and workshops from students:

*This class, archetypal drama, has brought psychology out of the books and into life. I have greatly enjoyed evoking the archetypes to see what form they are taking in our lives. For the first three weeks, I left every class at the end of the day shaking to the bone. I have left many classes inspired but never so moved to the very core of my being. This work is vital.*

*This was a journey of magic, of mystery, of power, of healing, of pain, of joy, of transcendence.*

*This was a great weekend for me. I was touched countless times by the work—there wasn't a single piece that didn't move me to tears....*

*It was like choreography—graceful, conscious but related, and an experience in how characters begin, grow and reconcile on this 'stage' set up in the classroom.*

*I'm feeling as though the universe has again bestowed an incredible gift into my heart and life and future. The form of this work is so powerful and yet so free to move in its purest energy.*

*I am inspired by the possibilities this work presents—it is amazing to me how profoundly transformational drama is and can be. Casting of roles seems to always reveal a deeper wisdom that is beyond our conscious minds.*

*In the universality of everyone's dramas, I found missing pieces of myself and was able to reconnect with them, own them, hear them and love them from that place of depth and compassion.*

❋

This, it seems to me, is generous homage to experiential learning that was born of this subtle alliance between the drama and the actively imaginative archetypal realm. Again and again, the energized imaginal integrity of particular archetypal dramas opened up for us and we responded. The drama engages figures, and sometimes entities hidden behind the figures. This is depth psychology pushed to new metaphorical measures, alive with complexity, paradox and the will to express emotion with largesse and excitement. Communion with the invisible becomes in Archetypal Drama a furtherance of all those ancient ideas about making the world complete through art and transformation, bringing into play the other, hidden world so that consciousness can meet its opposites, so that the soul can commune with its own elemental psychic depth, and thus live again in the immense matrix we call The Creative.

The throb of life returns, with pulses beating
Soft to ethereal dawn, O steadfast earth,
True through the night, you waited for my greeting,
Breathing beneath my feet in glad new birth,
And, clothing me afresh in joy of living,
In high resolve that banishes misgiving,
You stir my soul to prove life's utmost worth.

(Goethe's *Faust*: Part Two, Act I)

ꕤ

## ꧁ EPILOGUE ꧂

The stage is empty again. We have been involved in the structure of these dialogues, these dramatic excursions in the lives we have been living. The players who have meant so much to us have come and gone and we are again on our own, stretching the context, putting ourselves to rest before the next eventuality. This combining of elements for the sake of the soul we can call many things. It is an alchemy, a digestion, a play of oppositions, a run for the prize, a shuttle between two archetypal possibilities. It is probably foremost a liberating of subtle energized intelligence, the kind from which new worlds are formed. Perhaps it is time to begin again, trusting in our own momentum, going inside for another view, removing all imitative access from our mediated mentalities for the sake of a truer vision which includes beauty and meaning and perhaps a sacred character that is being imagined or written or enacted even now.

Bill Pearlman is a poet, actor, licensed therapist and program director of the Graduate Certificate in Archetypal Drama Therapy at Southwestern College in Santa Fe. He is the author of *Surfing Off the Ark (Poems 1965-1969), Inzorbital* (a novel also published by **d**uende **p**ress) and *Elegy for Prefontaine.* He is the director of the Institute for Archetypal Drama in Albuquerque. For information on Workshops in Archetypal Drama, write to the author, PO Box 613, Placitas, New Mexico 87043.

# REFERENCES

Artaud, Antonin. *The Theater And Its Double*. NY: Grove Press, 1958.

Avens, Roberts. *Imagination Is Reality*. Dallas: Spring, 1980.

Blatner, Adam and Alee. *The Art of Play*. NY: Human Sciences Press, 1988.

———. *Foundations of Psychodrama*. NY: Springer, 1988.

Bodkin, Maud. *Archetypal Patterns in Poetry*. London: Oxford University Press, 1934.

Brook, Peter. *The Empty Space*. NY: Avon, 1968.

Callow, Simon. *Being an Actor*. London: Meuthen, 1984.

Cassirer, Ernst. *An Essay on Man*. New Haven: Yale, 1944.

Cavell, Stanley. *Disowning Knowledge*. Cambridge: Univ. of Cambridge Press, 1987.

Chekov, Michael. *To the Actor*. New York: Barnes & Noble Books, 1985.

Coles, Toby. *Actors on Acting*. New York: Crown Publishers, 1970.

Corbin, Henry. *Creative Imagination in the Sufism of Ibn Arabi*. Bollingen Series XCI. Princeton Univ. Press, 1969.

Eliade, Mircea. *The Sacred and The Profane*. San Diego: Harcourt Brace, 1959.

Erikson, Erik. *Young Man Luther*. NY: Norton, 1964.

Flannery, James. *W.B. Yeats and the Idea of a Theatre*. Toronto: Macmillan, 1976.

Freud, Sigmund. *Complete Works*. NY: Norton, 1976.

Gelb, Arthur and Barbara Gelb, eds. *O'Neill*. NY: Harper, 1973.

George, G. & Karp, B. (Producer), & Malle, L. (Director). *My Dinner with Andre* [Film] Pacific Arts Video, Carmel, Ca., 1981.

Goldman, Michael. *The Actor's Freedom*. NY: Simon & Schuster, 1975.

Grotowski, Jerzy. *Towards a Poor Theatre*. NY: Simon & Schuster, 1968.

Havel, Vaclav. *Letters to Olga*. NY: Holt, 1989.

Hillman, James. *The Dream and the Underworld*. NY: Harper, 1979.

————. *Re-Visioning Psychology*. NY: Harper, 1975.

————. *Healing Fiction*. Barrytown, NY: Station Hill, 1983.

Humbert, Elie. *C.G. Jung: The Fundamentals of Theory & Practice*. Willmette, Illinois: Chiron, 1988.

Jung, C.G. *The Collected Works of C.G. Jung*. 20 vols. Translated by RFC Hull. Bollingen Series XX. Princeton University Press, 1957-79.

Kelly, George. *The Psychology of Personal Constructs*. 2 vols. NY: Norton, 1955.

McNiff, Shaun. *The Depth Psychology of Art*. Springfield, Illinois: C. Thomas, 1989.

Monte, Christopher. *Beneath the Mask*. Forth Worth: Harcourt Brace, 1991.

Moreno, J.L. *Psychodrama*, vol. 1. NY: Beacon, 1977.

Neumann, Eric. *Art and the Creative Unconscious*. Princeton: Bollingen, 1959.

Otto, Walter. *Dionysus*. Dallas: Spring, 1981.

Parkin, Andrew. *The Dramatic Imagination of W.B. Yeats.* Dublin: Gill and Macmillan, 1978.

Scheckner, Richard. *Performance Theory.* New York: Routledge, 1988.

Shakespeare, William. *The Riverside Shakespeare.* Boston: Houghton-Mifflin, 1974.

Smith and Berg. *Paradoxes of Group Life.* San Francisco: Jossey Bass, 1987.

Turner, Victor. *From Ritual to Theatre.* NY: Performing Arts Journal Publications, 1982.

Wiles, Timothy. *The Theatre Event.* Chicago: University of Chicago, 1980.

Willet, John. *Brecht On Theatre.* New York: Hill and Wang, 1964.

Winnicott, D.W. *Playing and Reality.* New York: Basic Books, 1971.

Yeats, W.B. *The (Variorum) Plays of W.B. Yeats.* NY: Macmillan, 1966.

————. *Autobiography.* NY: Doubleday, 1958.

————. *Explorations.* NY: Macmillan, 1962.

*Cover Design* Lenore Goodell
*Text* Zapf Calligraphic
*Paper* Recycled